O Come,
EMMANUEL

Published by
The Bible Reading Fellowship
First Floor, Elsfield Hall
15–17 Elsfield Way, Oxford OX2 8FG
Website: www.brf.org.uk

ISBN 1 84101 390 0
First published 2005
10 9 8 7 6 5 4 3 2 1 0

Acknowledgments

Unless otherwise stated, scripture quotations are taken from The New Revised
Standard Version of the Bible, Anglicized Edition, copyright © 1989, 1995 by the
Division of Christian Education of the National Council of the Churches of Christ in
the USA, and are used by permission. All rights reserved.

Extracts from the Authorized Version of the Bible (The King James Bible), the rights
in which are vested in the Crown, are reproduced by permission of the Crown's
patentee, Cambridge University Press.

'Wait for the Lord' copyright © Ateliers et Presses de Taizé, F—71250 Taizé-
Community, France. Printed with permission.

'Born in the night' by Geoffrey Ainger, reproduced by permission of Stainer & Bell
Ltd, London, England.

'Like a candle flame' by Graham Kendrick, copyright © 1988 Make Way Music,
info@makewaymusic.com. International copyright secured. All rights reserved.
Used by permission.

A catalogue record for this book is available from the British Library

Printed in Singapore by Craft Print International Ltd

O Come,
EMMANUEL

Reflections on music and readings
for Advent and Christmas

GORDON GILES

Acknowledgments

I wish to record my gratitude to all those who have assisted with and encouraged the writing of this book, during what turned out to be a very busy and exciting year. The congregation of St Mary Magdalene, Windmill Hill, Enfield have sampled some of the course material and inspired some of my thinking. From my father Graham I have learnt a love of music from an early age, but also scrounged scores and recordings for this and other projects. My friend and colleague Stuart Young has provided a haven of peace for quiet study and creativity. To all these people I offer heartfelt thanks.

The greater gratitude must go to my wife Jessica, who throughout the gestation of this book was playing the central part in our own nativity story. Her unstinting support was combined with the impending and then delivered reality of our daughter Maria, whose birth we hailed with great delight and thanksgiving, and to whom this book is lovingly dedicated: 'For unto us a child is born! Alleluia!'

CONTENTS

Introduction 7

December

1   The Advent responsory (Matthew 25:31–33, 41–46) 11
2   Come, thou redeemer of the earth (Isaiah 9:6–7) 16
3   Christus vincit (Revelation 11:15–18) 22
4   Lo! he comes with clouds descending (Revelation 1:3–8) 27
5   Wait for the Lord (1 Thessalonians 5:4–11) 33
6   St Nicholas (1 Timothy 3:1–7) 38
7   This is the record of John (Luke 1:68–79)...................................44
8   Thou whose almighty word (Luke 12:35–38) 49
9   Earth was waiting, spent and restless (Romans 8:18–25) 53
10 People, look east (Isaiah 60:1–5)...58
11 Born in the night (Isaiah 59:20–60:5) 64
12 The lamb (John 1:29–37) 69
13 Santa Lucia (Matthew 5:14–16)..74
14 Of the father's heart begotten (Matthew 1:1–17).......................78
15 This is the truth sent from above
    (Genesis 2:7, 15–18, 21–25)..84
16 Adam lay ybounden (Genesis 3:1–8) 89
17 O come, O come, Emmanuel!
    (Isaiah 7:4; 11:10; 22:22, Malachi 4:2)......................................94
18 Veni, veni, Emmanuel (Luke 21:20–28) 100
19 Once in royal David's city (Luke 2:1–7).....................................105
20 Gabriel's message (Luke 1:26–38) 110
21 Ave Maria (Luke 1:39–45) 114
22 Masters in this hall (Luke 1:46–55) 119
23 The cherry tree carol (Matthew 1:18–25) 125
24 Hark! the herald angels sing (Luke 2:8–14) 130
25 While shepherds watched their flocks (Luke 2:15–20) 136
26 Good King Wenceslas (Matthew 25:34–40)................................141

27 The candle song (John 1:1–9) 146
28 The Coventry carol (Matthew 2:16–18) 151
29 The childhood of Christ (Matthew 2:13–15)................156
30 In the bleak mid-winter (Philippians 2:5–11) 161
31 Christmas oratorio (Hebrews 1:1–6)..............................167

January

1   What child is this? (Matthew 2:1–6) 172
2   The twelve days of Christmas (Part 1)
    (Esther 9:17, 19–22) 178
3   A new dial (The twelve days of Christmas, Part 2) 183
4   Tomorrow shall be my dancing day
    (Ecclesiastes 3:1–8, 11)..189
5   Ahmal and the night visitors (Luke 4:14–22) 195
6   We three kings (Matthew 2:7–11) 200

Suggestions for group discussion or individual reflection 205

INTRODUCTION

Christmas is the most musical season of the year. At no other time do we sing or listen to so much music. Carol services and concerts provide a wealth of Christmas fare, as do troops of carol singers traipsing from door to door. Our shopping precincts often welcome carol singers at this time of year, and most radio stations enter into the seasonal spirit, broadcasting carols or Christmas-themed pop songs. The famous song 'Do they know it's Christmas?', originally released in 1984 after Bob Geldof KMG was inspired to raise money for Ethiopian famine victims, has maintained a place at the heart of the season for many (it became the greatest-selling UK single). It was re-recorded in 2004 (the 20th anniversary), once again begging the very question it purports to ask (*do* they know it's Christmas?). Whether people know it's Christmas or not, there is plenty of music to remind us, some of which also helps us to understand its meaning and message. Christmas is about the birth of Christ, even though there are people who do not know this, have forgotten it, or want to make it mean something different. And we have very little excuse for not knowing what Christmas is about, because so much of the music that we encounter at this time of year tells and interprets the events of the nativity in song.

Singing carols or attending concerts can be great fun, and for many, Christmas simply isn't Christmas without doing so. But Christmas is not about carols: carols are about Christmas! Those carols can teach and show us a great deal about our faith and can help us in our pilgrimage through life, reminding, cajoling and inspiring us to take the incarnation of Jesus seriously and to live our lives in the marvellous light of the love that God shows us by sending Jesus to us as saviour.

Over the next few weeks, we shall explore some of the Christmas music that we hear all too often, and some that may be unfamiliar. Whatever the scope or duration of the work, the music says something to us about the text and the text helps us understand what is going on musically. When the text is a sacred text (from the Bible or a prayer book), there comes into play another, deeper dimension as the composer tries to combine words and music either to praise God or to say something about God, or both. Day by day, using Advent and Christmas music, we will strive to magnify the wonders of God revealed in Jesus Christ, who is judge, redeemer, promised saviour, suffering servant, anointed one, king of glory, child of Bethlehem, Son of Man, Word made flesh, light of the world, lamb of God, incarnate Son of God.

As we read, we shall encounter ancient poetry and music preserved as hymns. We shall consider the words and tunes of some of the famous Christmas carols that we sometimes sing without a passing thought. (Even the tunes have names that they have been given by their composers, perhaps for a theological reason, or merely to associate them with a favourite place.) We will meet Christians from the past, and living poets and musicians of faith. In their words we find profound spiritual insight but also questionable theology, mystical wonder and pagan influence. We will dance with Christ, and walk with the wise men. We will travel to Turkey, Italy, Sweden, Germany, France and Spain on our route to the cradle at Bethlehem. And then we will flee from Herod to Coventry, although our apparently bleak midwinter will still be warmed by the sun of righteousness.

We will delve into Testaments Old and New, and manuscripts ancient and modern, in search of the truth from above. We will have fun and games with 12 partridges, 22 turtle doves, 30 French hens, 36 calling birds, 40 gold rings, 42 laying geese, 42 swans, 40 milk-maids, 36 dancing girls, 30 lords, 22 pipers and 12 drummers eventually in attendance! We will hear of selfless sacrifice, charity and love, of forgiveness, reconciliation and hope; yet we will also face the realities of death and judgment, pain and loss, crime and punishment, anticipation and disappointment, darkness and light.

With scripture and song, we will pray with confidence and fear, sorrow and joy, for others and ourselves. And, as is inevitable at this time of year, we will remember all those whom we love but see no longer, mindful of the fragility of human existence and the vastness of creation.

We know that our world is blessed with beauty but is also bombarded with brutality. The paradoxes of life come into particular focus during Advent, and it is the way we handle Advent that determines how and if we enjoy Christmas. As every year comes and goes, the feast of the nativity looks more and more like a feast and less like an incarnation. 'Hark! The herald angels sing' must become more of an instruction each year: 'Listen up, folks, Christmas is here, and it means something wonderful!' God's singular melody of Christmas, proclaimed by angels, is so easily drowned out by the cacophony of consumerism, with its overtones of overindulgence.

Christmas is a soft target for those who want to discredit faith, but for most people it is anticipated as a positive time of year, and in spite of the moans of the naysayers, millions do have a 'good Christmas', and there is much care and thought for those who are less fortunate. In churches we often have Christingle services and toy services, where gifts and money are collected for the disadvantaged. The lowest common denominator for Christmas is 'peace and goodwill', and in many circumstances, society demands and achieves much higher values, which find their basis in a heritage that some people still call 'Christian'. Whether or not people still 'believe' the message of Christmas, that God so loved the world that he sent his only Son Jesus into the world so that all may be saved (see John 3:16), the spirit of goodwill that many associate with this divine gesture of supreme love can still be found. Goodwill and charity are outward signs of faith in action, but in today's world we often see them even when the faith of which they might be symptomatic is absent. Christmas has become a time for works without faith, so much so that every year preachers and church leaders strive to put Christ back into Christmas. As we shall see, Christmas music provides a wonderful resource for doing just that.

So many people love Christmas carols, and sing them heartily in concerts, pubs and social gatherings, but how many people understand or believe what they are singing? Christmas carols are not nursery rhymes, even if they may be treated as such. Rather they speak of eternal truths and real events, significant even to our age, and remembered still.

While Advent, Christmas and Epiphany are very much part of our Christian heritage, having something of a Christian tradition and being familiar with and appreciative of it is not the same thing. In this book we can examine only a small part of the heritage of faith that forms the structure upon which these seasons are piled. Of course there are omissions: the season is simply not long enough to enable us to enjoy the full fare on offer. Nevertheless, it is my hope and prayer that this musical mystery tour of Advent and Christmas will help and inspire all of us to re-examine and notice what we sing and hear at this time of year.

As we venture into the season of Advent, and from there to Christmas and Epiphany, accompanied by a diverse group of musicians and poets, let us look for inspiration, hope, solace and encouragement and remember that our ultimate desire is the praise of God, creator Father, incarnate Son and living Spirit, not only at this time of year, but always.

THE ADVENT RESPONSORY

'When the Son of Man comes in his glory, and all the angels with him, then he will sit on the throne of his glory. All the nations will be gathered before him, and he will separate people one from another as a shepherd separates the sheep from the goats, and he will put the sheep at his right hand and the goats at the left... Then he will say to those at his left hand, "You that are accursed, depart from me into the eternal fire prepared for the devil and his angels; for I was hungry and you gave me no food, I was thirsty and you gave me nothing to drink, I was a stranger and you did not welcome me, naked and you did not give me clothing, sick and in prison and you did not visit me." Then they also will answer, "Lord, when was it that we saw you hungry or thirsty or a stranger or naked or sick or in prison, and did not take care of you?" Then he will answer them, "Truly I tell you, just as you did not do it to one of the least of these, you did not do it to me." And these will go away into eternal punishment, but the righteous into eternal life.'

MATTHEW 25:31–33, 41–46

I look from afar:
And lo, I see the power of God coming,
and a cloud covering the whole earth.

Go ye out to meet him and say:
Tell us, art thou he that should come to reign over thy people Israel?

High and low, rich and poor, one with another,
Go ye out to meet him and say:

Hear, O thou shepherd of Israel, thou that leadest Joseph like a sheep:
Tell us, art thou he that should come?

Stir up thy strength, O Lord, and come
To reign over thy people Israel.

Glory be to the Father, and to the Son, and to the Holy Ghost.
I look from afar, and lo, I see the power of God coming, and a cloud
covering the whole earth.

Go ye out to meet him and say:
Tell us, art thou he that should come to reign over thy people Israel?

WORDS: THE FIRST MATINS RESPONSORY FOR ADVENT SUNDAY
MUSIC: ADAPTED FROM G.P. DA PALESTRINA (C.1525–94)

The singing of this responsory at the beginning of an Advent carol service on the first Sunday of Advent marks the beginning of the December season of penitence, anticipation and hope. The words and music are derived from the doxology and chanted portions from the odd verses of the *Magnificat (Third Tone)* by Palestrina (the Bible text of the Magnificat is Luke 1:46–55). The responsory text itself comes from the old Latin service of Mattins (Morning Prayer). The version that has become popular through use at places such as King's College Chapel, Cambridge, has harmonized responses. It is then usual to lead straight into the ancient hymn 'Come, thou redeemer of the earth' (see 2 December, p. 16).

This simple opening to Advent points us towards the return of Christ as judge and king, reigning over the whole earth, but also judging the whole earth, as the parable of the sheep and goats suggests. For some, that judgment will not have satisfactory results. Surprising as it may seem, the idea of eternal judgment can still grab the headlines, in which every now and again we see phrases like 'Gone but not forgiven' or 'Gone to hell'. Such headlines appeared when Myra Hindley, the convicted child-killer, who had been in prison since the mid-1960s, died in November 2002. In a general population that pays little heed to any notion of judgment or salvation, and generally believes that heaven and hell are medieval fantasies, there occasionally appears a remarkable desire to cast certain notorious individuals into that eternal torture chamber that we have come to call hell. But this desire to ensure someone's safe passage into hell says far more about those wishing it than it does about the person whom they hate.

Similarly, we are, as a society, quite content to wish our loved ones into heaven—content to wish them into the 'next room' that Canon Henry Scott Holland called death (in a passage entitled 'Death is nothing at all')—and our thinking and believing about heaven is just as muddled and equally irrational. The logic of this irrationality is supreme: if religion is irrational, as it is thought to be, then anything irrational must be religious. This kind of religious feeling, which often raises its head when someone loved or hated dies, is mostly based upon the exercise of an emotional will, rather than on any rational theology. If we liked someone, we wish them well in the afterlife. If we disliked them, we wish them ill, and our wishes can so easily become our beliefs.

The Bible says that when we die we are judged. Advent is the distinctive season for reflecting on the last judgment, which Matthew describes in the parable of the sheep and the goats. In that parable we are presented with a kingly Christ as judge. This means that it is his criteria, not ours, which form the basis of that judgment. It is Christ who has the power, not us, and this actually means that he can do whatever he likes, but not in the sense that we can think what we 'like' when it comes to death and judgment. We believe that God was in Christ reconciling the world to himself, offering forgiveness, rescuing us from sin, and preparing a place for us in heaven. Therefore we have to acknowledge that when Christ sits on his heavenly throne, he can, and perhaps will, be very merciful indeed.

It would not be truly biblical of us to confine ourselves to an image of Christ sitting on a throne wielding absolute power. Christ is powerful, of course, but the Gospels are not a catalogue of his exercising worldly, judgmental power. They are rather accounts of how he shows that he has power, and, through his ministry, how he gently, bravely and *willingly* lays it down. We are shown, in the account of his temptations in the wilderness (Matthew 4:1–11), that Jesus had the power to be a very different kind of king—a tyrant who exercises absolute authority, governing through fear and the suppression of any alternative. But he rejected that approach, and it is fundamental to Christianity that we have a choice. Our king forces no allegiance from us, but frees us to love him, or not to do so.

In his earthly ministry, Jesus demonstrates his power to heal: cleansing lepers, casting out demons, curing the sick and lame. We also see Jesus' intellectual power. He tells parables and confounds the religious leaders of his time both by asking awkward questions of his own and by evading theirs. Whether it is tax to Caesar or the fate of a sinner, Jesus conquers their cunning and prejudice. This also reveals his moral power, as does the idea that he is sinless, both in character and action:

'Since, then, we have a great high priest who has passed through the heavens, Jesus, the Son of God, let us hold fast to our confession. For we do not have a high priest who is unable to sympathize with our weaknesses, but we have one who in every respect has been tested as we are, yet without sin' (Hebrews 4:14–15).

As we consider the end of Jesus' ministry, we realize, as his disciples do, that this is the Messiah (Luke 9:20), in whom all things were made, whose name is above all names in this age and in every age to come. Yet, as soon as we realize this, we see it all slip away. Betrayal, arrest, trials, torture, execution all follow in swift succession. Where has his power gone? He has laid it down—surrendered it to human hatred. He, who is characterized as the Son of Man judging humans like sheep and goats, allows himself to be humanly judged, falsely convicted and killed.

This kind of kingship and this kind of love are unique in history. This is the love of Christ, which inverts itself for the benefit of others, truly nourishing others. This kingship and this love are both about self-giving and the laying down of worldly power. That is why, if we want to think of Christ as a king, we must think of him not only as judge but primarily as the king of love. And it is the king of love whose return we anticipate and desire, not just in Advent, but at all times.

Prayer

As Advent begins, O Lord Christ, come again to reign over your people and enlighten all nations. Have mercy on all who look to you, and hasten that day when your justice and love will be revealed for the good of all creation and the glory of God the Father, with whom and the Spirit you are sovereign in majesty and power. Amen.

COME, THOU REDEEMER
OF THE EARTH

For a child has been born for us, a son given to us; authority rests upon his shoulders; and he is named Wonderful Counsellor, Mighty God, Everlasting Father, Prince of Peace. His authority shall grow continually, and there shall be endless peace for the throne of David and his kingdom. He will establish and uphold it with justice and with righteousness from this time onwards and for evermore. The zeal of the Lord of hosts will do this.

ISAIAH 9:6–7

Come, Thou Redeemer of the earth,
And manifest Thy virgin birth:
Let every age adoring fall;
Such birth befits the God of all.

Begotten of no human will,
But of the Spirit, Thou art still
The Word of God in flesh arrayed,
The promised Fruit to man displayed.

The virgin womb that burden gained
With virgin honour all unstained;
The banners there of virtue glow;
God in His temple dwells below.

Forth from His chamber goeth He,
That royal home of purity,
A giant in twofold substance one,
Rejoicing now His course to run.

From God the Father He proceeds,
To God the Father back He speeds;
His course He runs to death and hell,
Returning on God's throne to dwell.

O equal to the Father, Thou!
Gird on Thy fleshly mantle now;
The weakness of our mortal state
With deathless might invigorate.

Thy cradle here shall glitter bright,
And darkness breathe a newer light,
Where endless faith shall shine serene,
And twilight never intervene.

All laud to God the Father be,
All praise, eternal Son, to Thee;
All glory, as is ever meet,
To God the Holy Paraclete.

WORDS: AMBROSE OF MILAN (340–397), TRANS. JOHN MASON NEALE (1818–66)
MUSIC: *VENI REDEMPTOR* PLAINSONG MODE 1
PUER NOBIS NASCITUR TRIER MANUSCRIPT, 15TH CENTURY,
ADAPTED BY MICHAEL PRAETORIUS (1571–1621), 1609

'Come, Thou Redeemer of the earth' often follows the Advent Responsory, which we considered yesterday. That set of responses concludes with a D major chord, which sets the key for this hymn. Often the responsory is sung at the west end of the church, and then the choir proceed eastwards, singing this straightforward tune. It is a very effective way to open a service, with music and movement. As the choir walk eastwards, they are walking in the direction of Jerusalem, towards the chamber of salvation, the 'royal home' from which the Father sends his Spirit-begotten Son. Such a progression sets the scene for what is to follow: words and song telling forth the Advent promise of hope and light.

This carol is, as they say, one of the oldest ones in the book. Its author, Ambrose of Milan (*Ambrogio* in Italian), was not actually Italian but was born in Augusta Trevorum, which was then in Gaul (France), and is now known as Trier, in Germany. Hence he was a Roman citizen, who followed his father into a career in politics, being made governor of Aemilia-Liguria (northern Italy) around 370. When the bishop of Milan died in 374, the local lay people wanted Ambrose to succeed him. There was a major problem: Ambrose, while a believer, had not actually been ordained, or even baptized. After much soul-searching, he accepted the bishopric, and was hastily baptized and ordained. He became famous for his preaching and his role in the conversion of Augustine of Hippo (354–430). He wrote treatises on ethics and on the sacraments, and some have even attributed the Athanasian creed to his pen. Revered as a saint and a 'doctor' of the church, his feast day is 7 December in both Roman Catholic and Anglican calendars.

This hymn, known originally in Latin as *Veni, Redemptor gentium*, dates from 397, the last year of Ambrose's life, and was brought into English use by the Victorian poet and translator J.M. Neale, who, in his short life, made a very significant contribution to English hymnody of the 19th century. 'Good King Wenceslas' is one of his own compositions, but he is better known for his many hundred translations from Latin and Greek. The usual version of *Veni, Redemptor gentium* actually begins with the second verse: the first verse began '*Intende, qui regis Israel...*' ('You who are enthroned upon the cherubim, shine forth before Ephraim and Benjamin and Manasseh. Stir up your might, and come to save us!'), and is rarely heard today. The fourth and fifth verses were translated to echo the Book of Common Prayer version of Psalm 19:5: 'In them hath he set a tabernacle for the sun: which cometh forth as a bridegroom out of his chamber, and rejoiceth as a giant to run his course.' The first German version of this hymn was translated by a 15th-century clergyman from Freiburg, Henrik von Laufenberg, and then, in 1524, the reformer Martin Luther translated what is still known as 'Nun komm, der Heiden Heiland'. J.S. Bach used the plainsong melody in five chorales and in the Advent cantatas 36, 61 and 62.

Like Ambrose himself, the 16th-century tune PUER NOBIS NASCITUR came from Trier. (It has also been found in a 14th-century German manuscript, the Moosburg Gradual, and the 16th-century Finnish collection Piae Cantiones). The original words were 'Puer nobis nascitur, Rector angelorum' ('Unto us is born a child, guardian of the angels'), a slightly different version of which is the English hymn 'Unto us a boy is born'. The 16th-century German composer Michael Praetorius adapted the version most often used for 'Come, Thou Redeemer of the earth'. Praetorius means 'mayor' in Latin, and Michael Schultheiss (or Shultz) is known to history by that name. He was a theologian as well as a musician, studying at the university in Frankfurt an der Oder (the 'other' Frankfurt) while also working as an organist. By 1595 he was working for Duke Heinrich Julius von Braunschweig, initially as organist and then as Master of Music.

In 1613, Praetorius moved to Dresden to work for the Elector of Saxony, but after two years he returned home, becoming a peripatetic organizer of musical events and general adviser to any who required his services. He was also a musical editor, publishing a nine-volume collection of over 1200 arrangements of hymns and songs, and a three-part work of musical history and criticism. He is largely to be credited with the authorship or collation of much of the North German Lutheran church's basic liturgical musical repertoire. (For a wonderful example of his work, listen to Paul McCreesh's 1994 reconstruction of a Lutheran Christmas Mass, with Praetorius' music, DG Archiv 439 250–2.)

As we proceed into Advent, with Christmas as our destination, it is good to have a sketch map of the terrain ahead. And what a reminder! Here in microcosm we have the desire of nations expressed: 'Come, redeemer of the earth' and the anticipation of the virgin birth at Bethlehem, both in the first verse. We are reminded that the incarnate Christ, although born at a point in space and time, is still the Son of God. Christ reigns in glory as the Word made flesh, and dwells among us today in the ministry of the Holy Spirit. Ambrose refers to Christ as the 'promised fruit', a lovely description which recalls the 'forbidden fruit' that tempts Adam and Eve, but which also hails Christ as the promised Saviour anticipated by Isaiah and in the Psalms. Christ, the second Adam, turns forbidden fruit into promised fruit, fulfilling the pages of prophecy and bringing release to all those who, like the first Adam, are bound by sin.

The use of the word 'fruit' is also reminiscent of the description of Jesus as 'fruit of the womb of Mary' (Luke 1:42), and Ambrose writes of Jesus 'coming forth' from the chamber that is his mother's womb, the 'royal place of purity'. Thus, from her is born a child, both human and divine. The fourth-century poetry is earthy and earthly, but in being so it combines the mystery of incarnation with the real presence of human birth.

In this rich passage of poetry there is much condensed, so that only hints of Isaiah's words of promise can be detected. Ambrose's deep theological insight encapsulates the promise and realization of salvation in Christ, whose birth is foreseen in Isaiah 9 and described in Luke 1—2. Thus his hymn is a treatise in itself, to which he brings a lifetime of spiritual study and pastoral wisdom. In this one hymn, he succeeds in doing something to which we devote the whole Advent carol service: unpacking the prophetic meaning of certain Old Testament passages and the gradual realization that they point to and predict the birth and ministry of Christ.

A hymn as ancient as this reminds us of the journey already travelled by those as far back as Ambrose, who, holding the faith that we grasp centuries later, articulated his theology and his adoration in words that speak in the midst of today's completely different social and ecclesiastical context. Plainsong melodies and chants still resonate across time, reminding us that however different the vision of our spiritual ancestors may have been, they still lived and prayed in adoration and gratitude for the incarnation of their Saviour, and our Saviour, Jesus Christ our Lord—and hope for his return.

Prayer

O Lord our redeemer, whose incarnation manifests the love of the Father revealed in human flesh, breathe a new light upon your world, that the weakness of our mortality might be invigorated by your power and glory, until that day when all nations will bow down before your throne, on which you reign, Father, Son and Holy Spirit, now and for ever. Amen.

CHRISTUS VINCIT

Then the seventh angel blew his trumpet, and there were loud
voices in heaven, saying, 'The kingdom of the world has become
the kingdom of our Lord and of his Messiah, and he will reign
for ever and ever.' Then the twenty-four elders who sit on their
thrones before God fell on their faces and worshipped God,
singing, 'We give you thanks, Lord God Almighty, who are and
who were, for you have taken your great power and begun to reign.
The nations raged, but your wrath has come, and the time for
judging the dead, for rewarding your servants, the prophets and
saints and all who fear your name, both small and great, and for
destroying those who destroy the earth.'
REVELATION 11:15–18

Christ conquers,
Christ is King,
Christ is the Lord.

O Christ, hear us.
To the Holy Church of God, uniting
souls across the divisions of the nations: perpetual peace!

Christ conquers...
King of kings. Our King.
Our hope. Our glory.

O Christ, hear us.
To all leaders of the nations, and
those entrusted to their care;
honour unstained, life and victory.

O Christ, hear us.
O King of the nations, and their
desire, the Corner-stone,
who makest both one.

Christ conquers…
Our aid.
Our strength.
Our invincible shield.
Our impregnable wall.
Our light, our way, and our life.

O Christ, hear us.
O Emmanuel, our King and
lawgiver, the goal of all nations
and their Saviour.

Christ conquers…
To him alone be the sovereignty,
praise and rejoicing, through
unending ages of ages. Amen.

May they have happiness,
Who are redeemed by the
blood of Christ! And joy!
May Christ's peace come!
May Christ's kingdom come!
Thanks be to God. Amen.

LAUDES REGIAE: WORDS AND CHANT ELEVENTH CENTURY (OR EARLIER)

This very ancient piece of music was originally used in French monasteries and churches when the king attended worship. An early manuscript is associated with Osmund, who, as bishop of Salisbury (then known as Sarum) in the eleventh century, completed the building of the cathedral there. His mother, Lady Isabella of Normandy, was half-sister to William the Conqueror. After the invasion of 1066, he was supposedly made Earl of Dorset or Somerset, and also became Castellan of Old Sarum, but then became a priest and royal chaplain before being promoted to Chancellor in 1072. He was instrumental in the compilation of the Domesday Book, and in 1078 he became the first bishop of Salisbury.

Osmund is credited with the 'Ordinal of Offices', which, as the 'Sarum Rite', became widely used as the primary liturgical service book throughout the south of England. The original is still preserved in Salisbury Cathedral, as is a copy of the *Laudes Regiae*. Osmund himself was buried in the old Sarum cathedral, and his body was moved to the present medieval cathedral after it was completed in 1258. Accredited with various miracles, he was canonized in 1456.

Christus Vincit, which is also known as the *Laudes Regiae*, is thought to date from eighth-century France. At that time, it was usual for the king to visit Notre Dame cathedral during Advent in order to bring a gift, and also on Easter Sunday (it is not clear whether the *Laudes Regiae* was sung on both occasions, although the text given above contains Advent references). Three canons sang the text, honouring kings, clergy, judges and soldiers. The purpose of these acclamations was to demonstrate to the people that the king was ruler on earth as Christ was the ruler of heaven. Eventually, the *Laudes Regiae* was sung after the Mass that accompanied coronations.

Musically, it is based on a plainchant melody, but it can properly be called an early Latin motet. The lower (tenor) voice sings a fragment from an Easter chant, 'This is the day that the Lord has made' (*Haec dies*), while the upper part sings faster notes with text. Medieval motets were compositions based on a chant sung by a tenor voice, with one or more other voices singing additional texts commenting on or embellishing the original. They are called 'motets' from the French *mot* (meaning 'word').

While the impact and meaning of *Christus Vincit* is strong and regal, it can be both appealing and disturbing. In history it has been used to uphold and defend the power of kings, by allying their power to the power of Christ the King. How are we to understand or engage with the so-called kingship of Christ? There aren't very many kings to relate to these days, and while there are reigning kings in various countries, they are generally constitutional monarchs, having little real power, serving as symbolic heads of state. In the past, kingship has automatically been understood in terms of power and authority, and such authority was exercised in the name of God.

While the power of kings or queens is not something with which we are particularly familiar these days, we are very familiar with the concept of power, for all around us people are exercising power on many levels and in different contexts, for better or worse. Power is really all about change. The people in power are those who can bring about, or prevent, change. In order to do this, there can be exploitative power at play, where violence or threats are involved. There can also be manipulative power, such that the desire is to shape another person's or group's behaviour to suit one's own ends. This can happen at international level or at a quiet, personal level. There is also competitive power—the kind of power that is often felt and wielded in playgrounds and boardrooms alike.

There are also positive models of power, such as integrative power, which is exercised in order to support or underscore another's power. Integrative power backs other people up, defends them and stands alongside them, in sickness or in health, for better or worse. Integrative power creates a positive power base that is mutual and often outward-looking. This is a kind of fellowship power—strength in numbers, the power of trust and teamwork. It is the kind of power that Jesus exercised throughout his ministry as he taught and trained the disciples to carry on his work and spread the gospel after his resurrection and ascension.

There is another positive form of power, which sociologists call 'nutrient' power, which is power used on behalf of another's greater good. This sounds a bit like the power of love, the power of putting someone else first, or at least of putting one's own abilities, information, expertise and desires at the service of others. This is the power of giving, both of self and of resources.

These are certainly not the models of power that the eleventh-century Norman conquerors or their clergy had in mind. Today, to help us towards a more contemporary way of understanding Christ's kingship, we can think of these two kinds of power—integrative and nutrient power—remembering that Christ's kingship is unique and is in some sense paradoxical. Christ certainly has power, but his sovereignty consists largely in the fact that he gave it up when he submitted himself to the human, destructive wills that put him on a cross to die. Christ's sovereignty consists in weakness, belying a greater power. And that greater power is the power of divine love—love revealed, love laid down, love spent.

Prayer

O Christ our King, shine your light on our souls, that we may reflect your love. Deepen our vision, that we may see you more clearly. Refine us like gold, that we may become pure in your sight. Touch our hearts and lives, that we may always act for your sake, in the power of your love, for you lived and died for us, but now reign in glory. Amen.

LO! HE COMES WITH CLOUDS DESCENDING

Blessed is the one who reads aloud the words of the prophecy, and blessed are those who hear and who keep what is written in it; for the time is near.

John to the seven churches that are in Asia: Grace to you and peace from him who is and who was and who is to come, and from the seven spirits who are before his throne, and from Jesus Christ, the faithful witness, the firstborn of the dead, and the ruler of the kings of the earth. To him who loves us and freed us from our sins by his blood, and made us to be a kingdom, priests serving his God and Father, to him be glory and dominion for ever and ever. Amen.

Look! He is coming with the clouds; every eye will see him, even those who pierced him; and on his account all the tribes of the earth will wail. So it is to be. Amen. 'I am the Alpha and the Omega,' says the Lord God, who is and who was and who is to come, the Almighty.

REVELATION 1:3–8

> *Lo! he comes with clouds descending,*
> *Once for favoured sinners slain;*
> *Thousand thousand saints attending*
> *Swell the triumph of his train:*
> *Alleluya!*
> *God appears, on earth to reign.*

Every eye shall now behold him
Robed in dreadful majesty;
Those who set at nought and sold him,
Pierced and nailed him to the tree,
Deeply wailing
Shall the true Messiah see.

Those dear tokens of his passion
Still his dazzling body bears,
Cause of endless exultation
To his ransomed worshippers:
With what rapture
Gaze we on those glorious scars!

Yea, Amen! let all adore thee,
High on thine eternal throne;
Saviour, take the power and glory:
Claim the kingdom for thine own:
O come quickly!
Alleluya! Come, Lord, come!

WORDS: CHARLES WESLEY (1707–88) AND JOHN CENNICK (1718–55)
MUSIC: HELMSLEY. MELODY NOTATED BY THOMAS OLIVERS (1725–99)

Advent gives us an opportunity to focus on many important aspects of faith, and although the season is not as long as Lent, there are some common flavours. Advent, like Lent, is a penitential season, when we remind ourselves of our sinful nature, offering the season to God as a time for self-denial and improvement. We change the colour of robes and hangings in churches, and the clergy often wear the same purple garments as in Lent. Both are seasons of preparation: in Lent, for Easter; and in Advent we should prepare for the second coming of Christ. For many, Advent is about preparing for Christmas, and while the high street shops are very good at doing that for us, we must never lose sight of the fact that

Advent points us towards the return of our Saviour, not merely a remembrance of his incarnation two millennia ago.

This hymn, so often associated with Advent and rarely sung outside this season, is not necessarily best considered as purely appropriate for Advent. The words include 'Alleluya', a joyful outburst which some traditions exclude during Advent and Lent, as a sombre gesture in keeping with the penitential flavour of the season. Thus it can be strange singing this hymn if we have 'given up' alleluias for Advent! In other respects, though, this is an excellent Advent hymn, because it focuses on the second coming of Christ, which is often dwarfed by a pre-Christmas anticipation.

The opening lines are drawn from the book of Revelation and declare at the outset that this is no sugary Christmas carol but a hymn that relishes the return of our Lord. We are invited to look heavenwards, to see the promised Saviour returning, just as John prophesied in Revelation 1:3, echoing Daniel 7:13–15. And as he descends, the throng of the redeemed sweeps down to accompany his return in glory to earth, and those who nailed Jesus to the cross will at last see him as he is (1 John 3:2), the true Messiah. As the Messiah returns to judge, this may well cause those who have rejected him to 'wail deeply'. The image is a strong one, and we are introduced here to a scene of glory and power, but also of tribulation, pain and destruction. Such scenes are foretold by Jesus in Mark 13, Matthew 24 and Luke 21.

This apocalyptic element of Advent is one of the season's key themes. We live in a kind of middle time—a period after the incarnation, death and resurrection of Jesus, when God sent his Son into the world to carry the burden and weight of sin, so that he might open his arms for us on the cross, but also those days before the great end-time, when God shall bring all together. The end of the world is not something we generally want to contemplate, even though a basic knowledge of solar science indicates a future time when life on earth will not be sustainable. We can live in denial of such a future, and reconcile ourselves to the fact that it probably won't affect you or me, but we cannot actually deny the reality of

29

the end of the world, any more than we can deny its beginning.

There are two verses of this hymn which are seldom sung these days, written by John Cennick, whose hymn Wesley knew. Verse four of the text above, for example, is Wesley's adaptation of Cennick's poetry. These other verses run as follows:

> *Every island, sea and mountain,*
> *Heav'n and earth, shall flee away;*
> *All who hate Him must, confounded,*
> *Hear the trump proclaim the Day:*
> *Come to judgment!*
> *Come to judgment! Come away!*
>
> *Now redemption, long expected,*
> *See in solemn pomp appear!*
> *All His saints, by man rejected,*
> *Now shall meet him in the air:*
> *Alleluia!*
> *See the Day of God appear!*

These verses, it might be felt, do not add greatly to the theme of the hymn, but rather extend and elaborate it. Cennick's verses were amalgamated with Wesley's verses by Martin Madan (1726–90) to create a six-verse hymn, which itself has been often cut to produce the four-verse edition we frequently sing today. The final verse contains parts from both Wesley and Cennick, and the fifth verse, by Wesley, runs as follows:

> *Answer thine own Bride and Spirit,*
> *Hasten, Lord, the gen'ral Doom!*
> *The New Heav'n and Earth t'inherit,*
> *Take thy pining exiles home:*
> *All creation*
> *Travails! Groans! and bids Thee come!*

Like Cennick's, these words remind us of the challenge that 18th-century revivalism issued to believers: to look forward to the day of doom and glory, when Christ physically returns to claim his own.

The popular, rousing tune HELMSLEY is said to have been a favourite of Queen Victoria. Thomas Olivers originally wrote it for Wesley's hymn, but it was adapted by Martin Madan when he altered the words. Olivers was a Welsh cobbler who had been orphaned at the age of four, but his life changed when he heard the preaching of George Whitfield on a text from Zechariah 3:2 ('Is not this man a brand plucked from the fire?'). Olivers met John Wesley and became an itinerant preacher himself, initially in Cornwall, and in Wales. Wesley included this tune in his *Select Hymns* of 1765, and, despite various adaptations by Madan and others, it remains the main tune, even though others, such as REGENT SQUARE, have been tried.

Here, then, at the beginning of Advent, we have a rousing tune to accompany stirring words that demand a certain response. Widely sung as this hymn is, we can't help wondering how many people sing these words proclaiming the return of Christ, but lack any sense of the reality of such a proclamation. It is easy to sing about the return of Christ, but how much harder to believe it, and harder still to live in the light of passages of scripture such as the opening verses of the book of Revelation, which proclaim the return of Christ, who was and is and *is to come*.

As we move into the Advent season ourselves, we might begin by considering how we react to these apocalyptic visions. Do we believe them? Do we act and speak as though this kind of second coming might actually happen? In our imaginations do we gaze with rapture on Christ's dazzling body, singing 'Alleluia' and looking forward to the coming of his kingdom here on earth? And what do we feel about the possibility that it might happen tomorrow?

Prayer

Christ our true Messiah, we adore you, high on your eternal throne. Prepare us to accept that day when you claim your kingdom for your own, when you return in glory to confound all those who think of you as nothing more than an interesting historical figure. Come as judge, redeemer and mercy-giver, so that all tears may be wiped away and all wailing turned to rapture, for you live and reign, in union with the Father and the Spirit, now and for ever. Amen.

5 December

WAIT FOR THE LORD

But you, beloved, are not in darkness, for that day to surprise you like a thief; for you are all children of light and children of the day; we are not of the night or of darkness. So then, let us not fall asleep as others do, but let us keep awake and be sober; for those who sleep sleep at night, and those who are drunk get drunk at night. But since we belong to the day, let us be sober, and put on the breastplate of faith and love, and for a helmet the hope of salvation. For God has destined us not for wrath but for obtaining salvation through our Lord Jesus Christ, who died for us, so that whether we are awake or asleep we may live with him. Therefore encourage one another and build up each other, as indeed you are doing.

1 THESSALONIANS 5:4–11

Wait for the Lord, whose day is near,
Wait for the Lord, keep watch, take heart.
WORDS AND MUSIC: TAIZÉ COMMUNITY

It was a few years ago that I found myself really waiting for a thief to come in the middle of the night. I was visiting my parents at the time. One evening my father had his car stolen, and also a set of house keys, which meant that the thieves not only knew where he lived but also had the keys to the front door. We changed the locks, but the following morning we noticed a strange car driving past the house, with the people in it obviously having a good look round. We rang the police, who called back at 10.30 that night, saying that the car we had seen had been using false number plates; they thought they knew who had stolen the car (an established gang of thieves) and could we please move out of the house tonight so that they could lie in wait for the thieves to turn up?

As well as being a little surprising, this was also massively inconvenient as we didn't have anywhere to go at such short notice. The police then asked us to come to the police station in order to collect a plain-clothes officer, who would stay with us all night. My mother went out and soon returned with a very tall man wearing jeans, with handcuffs in his back pockets. He politely explained that we were to go to bed as normal, but he also told us that he was planning to spend the night *up a tree* opposite the house, and had we a scarf he could borrow? Also, could we open the back gate, which led into some woods, so that the other four policemen could slip in unnoticed? (This story is completely true, just in case you were wondering.) Soon enough, the others arrived, with body armour and armed with guns and those nasty long sticks that they use nowadays.

These five policemen were going to wait inside and outside the house, convinced that the thieves in the night were bound to come. If we stayed upstairs and just went to sleep, everything would be fine, and they would jump on the thieves as soon as they attempted to enter. Thus reassured, we showed the boys in blue where the teapot was, picked up our 60-kilo labrador dog who could no longer get up the stairs, and went to bed.

But absolutely nothing happened! No one came. There was no screeching of tyres, no struggle, no shots fired, no arrests. In a way, it was all very disappointing. And the next morning the only evidence of the previous night's adventure was a neatly folded scarf left at the bottom of the stairs.

Yet, while it was really rather frightening, it was also quite exciting in a strange kind of way: this was certainly a novel experience, and since we had some faith in our protectors, we almost hoped that the thieves would come. However, our waiting and the policemen's waiting were in vain. In that much, I suspect, we had something in common with the people of the early church, who believed that the second coming of Christ was imminent. They waited, partly in fear, partly in excitement, for something that did not happen and has not yet happened. Some of them were so confident that Jesus' return was imminent that they even gave up working. It is sometimes hard for us to appreciate that they were as certain that it would happen in their time as those policemen were confident that the thieves would turn up. It has so far not happened. The early church waited, and we, their spiritual descendants, continue to wait.

In the church, we traditionally associate waiting with this season of Advent. It is a time for pausing on our fast and hectic journey through life. One of the most effective ways to experience a sense of our Lord's return—to 'wait for the Lord'—comes through contemplative music and prayer. I'm sure it is no coincidence that the kind of gentle, repetitive, contemplative singing revived by the Taizé community in France has been successful and popular because it enables us to engage with our own waiting spaces. This can be true whether we listen to music at home or participate in services using this kind of music. Silence can be difficult to handle (some people definitely dislike it), but the music of Taizé has made a distinctive and vital contribution to the prayer lives of millions of people.

The Taizé community is not a commercial venture, nor does it insist upon a narrow doctrine to which its friends and members must adhere. Founded in wartime Burgundy by (Brother) Roger Schutz, a Swiss man who initially gave assistance to Jews fleeing Nazi Germany, the Taizé community grew after the war, spreading a message of reconciliation. By 1949, Roger had been ordained, and four Swiss and three French men took vows of celibacy, poverty and obedience, joining the community. Committed to ecumenical relations (the breaking down of divisions among Christian denominations), the Taizé community became popular with young people. Taizé is a place distinguished by its freedoms of spirit, fellowship and language, and most of all by its sense of community, which, although located firmly in France, is easily translatable to other places and contexts.

'Wait for the Lord' reminds us of another dimension of waiting that is typical of the Taizé approach to life and faith, for instead of the excitement, the fear and anticipation, there is also gentle acceptance and harmonious patience as we wait for the Lord. We have been waiting a long time, repeating the same basic melody, yet perhaps embellishing it creatively, so that our interest, our desire and our love are not wearied. The way Taizé chants are sung involves continuity and repetition combined with creativity and personality, expressed in communal worship. A simple melody is harmonized in a fairly straightforward way, which means that through repetition even inexpert singers can learn their own part in the greater musical whole. Sometimes 'canons' are used: divided groups sing the same tune a few notes apart, so that the melody keeps entering over again and the music seems overlaid, every part harmonizing with every other part.

The simple but effective approach to communal music and prayer both speaks to and reflects today's age in a beautifully integrated way. Each time we participate in a Taizé chant, we are involving ourselves in a stationary time with God, waiting for God and waiting with God. When we emerge from such an experience, we find that while time appears to have stood still, held in musical check by mutual melody, we ourselves have made a little journey towards God, accompanied by the Holy Spirit.

Advent is full of crime, of cops and robbers: both Paul, in our reading from 1 Thessalonians, and Luke (12:38–40) tell us that the second coming of Christ arrives 'like a thief in the night'. Waiting for God, if it is real waiting, is never boring, predictable or convenient. And in the time of waiting, we have an opportunity to reject the here-and-now of present living and engage with God over time, forming a deep and extended relationship, in the heart of which we can search and be searched out, know and be known. We not only wait *for* God, we wait *with* God. To do that takes time, but we do have time. Let us not waste it or lose it, for one day, inevitably, we will run out of time. And let us hope and pray that when we do, we will not be caught red-handed, like a couple of nocturnal burglars.

Prayer

God of day and night, keep us vigilant in faith and patient in praise, until that great day when Christ returns in clouds of glory to lift us to your heavenly throne. Amen.

ST NICHOLAS

The saying is sure: whoever aspires to the office of bishop desires a noble task. Now a bishop must be above reproach, married only once, temperate, sensible, respectable, hospitable, an apt teacher, not a drunkard, not violent but gentle, not quarrelsome, and not a lover of money. He must manage his own household well, keeping his children submissive and respectful in every way—for if someone does not know how to manage his own household, how can he take care of God's church? He must not be a recent convert, or he may be puffed up with conceit and fall into the condemnation of the devil. Moreover, he must be well thought of by outsiders, so that he may not fall into disgrace and the snare of the devil.

1 TIMOTHY 3:1–7

> *God moves in a mysterious way*
> *His wonders to perform;*
> *He plants his footsteps in the sea,*
> *And rides upon the storm.*
>
> *Deep in unfathomable mines*
> *Of never-failing skill*
> *He treasures up his bright designs,*
> *And works his sovereign will.*
>
> *Ye fearful saints, fresh courage take,*
> *The clouds ye so much dread*
> *Are big with mercy, and shall break*
> *In blessings on your head.*

Judge not the Lord by feeble sense,
But trust him for his grace;
Behind a frowning providence
He hides a smiling face.

His purposes will ripen fast,
Unfolding every hour;
The bud may have a bitter taste,
But sweet will be the flower.

Blind unbelief is sure to err,
And scan his work in vain;
God is his own interpreter,
And he will make it plain.

WORDS: WILLIAM COWPER (1731–1800)
MUSIC: LONDON NEW. MELODY FROM THE SCOTTISH PSALTER (1635),
ADAPTED IN *PLAYFORD'S PSALMES* (1671)

In many European countries, the feast of St Nicholas (Santa Claus) is celebrated today. Unlike the Swiss and Austrians (for example), English speakers do not generally make much of St Nicholas' Day, preferring to note in passing that he was bishop of Myra in the early fourth century. Myra is very close to the modern Turkish city of Demre, and it is in the basilica there that Nicholas was buried. In 1087 it was plundered by Italian sailors who took his remains to Bari in southern Italy, where his shrine still stands in the cathedral of St Nicholas. Controversy still rages about where St Nicholas' bones really are, or, indeed, whether they ought to be returned to his Turkish homeland.

By the sixth century, Nicholas had aroused a certain following, and in the ninth century Methodius of Constantinople articulated some of the legends that had sprung up about his life and works. By the 13th century, when Jacobus de Voragine collected together his *Legenda Sanctorum* (*Legend of the Saints*) between 1255 and 1266,

Nicholas' reputation was firmly established. His popularity was strong in England in the eleventh and twelfth centuries, largely because of the influence of the Archbishop of Canterbury, Anselm, and the long-lived hermit Godric, both of whom wrote poetry or prayers in Nicholas' honour. The *Legenda Sanctorum* was translated in 1450 and became one of the first books printed in English by William Caxton, under the title *The Golden Legend*. Interest in the book was revived in 1892 when William Morris reprinted it (see 22 December). By then, St Nicholas' name had evolved into Santa Claus, in American use, via the Dutch version of his name, *Sint Klaus*, and he became a figure of great interest. Connecting all the legends together was a recurring theme—of Nicholas' special patronage of sailors and of children.

Thus Nicholas was an ideal choice as the subject of a cantata for children's choir. The composer was Benjamin Britten (1913–76), whose friend, the tenor Peter Pears, had been a pupil at Lancing College in West Sussex. The college was celebrating its centenary in 1948, and Britten was commissioned to produce the work. The text was prepared by Eric Crozier, and although writing music for amateurs and children to perform presented particular difficulties, it also inspired Britten to produce a completely new type of musical work.

The part of Nicholas is taken by a tenor soloist, who gives us an insight into the ministry of an episcopal saint. He laments the condition of humanity and the prevalence of sin, but also accepts his own death with hope and courage. In the Introduction, we meet Nicholas, as though across time, who encourages us to preserve and teach the faith that still lives in us. The choir sing a prayer asking God for strength to serve.

Then we travel back 1600 years to 'The birth of Nicholas', where, apparently, his love of water, whether in bath or font, is manifest. Punctuating the movement is Nicholas' youthful cry, 'God be glorified', and at the end it is the tenor soloist, representing the adult saint, who takes up the call. This leads into a movement entitled 'Nicholas devotes himself to God'. Here he reflects on the poverty of humanity, destined to die in fear of everlasting death. Nicholas sells his land to feed the hungry but still has an 'angry soul'. Discordant music here gives way to musical resolution, telling us that God has heard his prayer.

The fourth movement, 'He journeys to Palestine', recounts a sea voyage. Nicholas predicts a storm, but is mocked by the crew. That night a storm does arise. The sailors are stricken and eventually turn to prayer. Nicholas joins them in praying for the storm to cease, and soon the waves are quelled and peace is restored. The movement ends as Nicholas thanks God for their deliverance. The fifth movement sees Nicholas arrive in Myra, where he is chosen as bishop. Then, in an unusual twist of convention, the audience stand to join in the well-known hymn, based on Psalm 100, 'All people that on earth do dwell'. This involvement of the audience turns them into a dramatic congregation—the flock for whom Nicholas is chief pastor.

In the sixth movement, 'Nicholas from prison', we meet Nicholas as a victim of Roman persecution. He has to celebrate communion with prison bread, but his fervour is still strong. He admonishes those who continue in sin, entreating them to bow down before God. Then, in the seventh movement, we move away from the prison as the choir tell of some travellers wandering without food. Three women call for Timothy, Mark and John, their missing sons. At an inn, the travellers order a meal, but Nicholas realizes that the meat they are to be served is actually the flesh of the three boys, who have been killed and pickled in salt. Nicholas calls them back to life and they enter, praising God and singing Alleluias.

Nicholas' good deeds are the subject of the eighth movement, 'His piety and marvellous works'. Now he is an old man, having been bishop for 40 years, and the choir sing of his devotion, courage and kindness. They remind us that he has saved them from imprisonment, hunger, shame, oppression and shipwreck. Nicholas is soon to die, and in the final movement, 'The death of Nicholas', he hears his call and looks forward to the eternal life of heaven in union with Christ. The Nunc Dimittis is sung (Luke 2:29–32), and as the sound swells, the organ gently introduces a final familiar hymn for everyone to sing: 'God moves in a mysterious way'. Thus the cantata closes with this reminder of how we can never fully understand the workings of God, yet we can trust in his mercy and rely on him to bring us through the storms of life.

Whether we celebrate the feast of St Nicholas or not, there can be no doubt that he existed, even if some of the legends about him are quite elaborate. In one sense, we must say that Father Christmas exists.

The difficulty today comes when Santa Claus (Father Christmas) is confused with Jesus, such that many agonize over whether or not to tell their children about Santa Claus bringing presents. Children write to him, and a whole industry has arisen around the plastic patron saint of present-giving. If Santa Claus and Jesus are too much associated, then there really is the risk that when children realize that Santa Claus is a modern commodity, they will throw the baby Jesus out with the bathwater-loving saint. A recent advertising campaign even portrayed Santa Claus in the manger, as a way of emphasizing the confusion that currently exists. 'Go on, ask him for something' read the caption. In that image lies the fundamental truth and purpose about Nicholas, for he, as a saint, would never have wanted the attention on himself but would have always desired to witness to Christ his Lord and Saviour. Santa Claus witnesses to Christ, and we must never forget that. The same is invariably true for bishops and church leaders today. Ordained as leaders in the church, just like Nicholas, they too have a daunting task of pastoral care and evangelism, and Timothy's description of the character of a bishop is no less relevant today. Such leaders of the church need and value our prayers.

Whether we are bishops, priests, deacons or laity, we should always tell children the truth about Santa Claus and, more importantly, the truth about Christ in the manger—Christ the baby born to become the man who was to die for our salvation. This is the true belief of Christmas, shared by you and me, and by Santa Claus himself.

Prayer

O God, the Father of Christmas, and of all time, send us your Holy Spirit, that we may be brought the gifts of love, joy and peace that you desire for your children in this and every age, for the sake of your Son, Jesus Christ our Lord. Amen.

THIS IS THE RECORD OF JOHN

Blessed be the Lord God of Israel,
for he has looked favourably on his people and redeemed them.
He has raised up a mighty saviour for us
in the house of his servant David,
as he spoke through the mouth of his holy prophets from of old,
that we would be saved from our enemies
and from the hand of all who hate us.
Thus he has shown the mercy promised to our ancestors,
and has remembered his holy covenant,
the oath that he swore to our ancestor Abraham,
to grant us that we, being rescued
from the hands of our enemies,
might serve him without fear, in holiness and righteousness
before him all our days.
And you, child, will be called the prophet of the Most High;
for you will go before the Lord to prepare his ways,
to give knowledge of salvation to his people
by the forgiveness of their sins.
By the tender mercy of our God,
the dawn from on high will break upon us,
to give light to those who sit in darkness
and in the shadow of death,
to guide our feet into the way of peace.

LUKE 1:68–79

This is the record of John, when the Jews sent priests and Levites from Jerusalem to ask him, Who art thou?

And he confessed, and denied not; and said plainly, I am not the Christ.

And they asked him, What art thou then? Art thou Elias? And he said, I am not. Art thou the prophet? And he answered, No.

Then said they unto him, What art thou? that we may give an answer unto them that sent us. What sayest thou of thyself?

And he said, I am the voice of him that cryeth in the wilderness, Make straight the way of the Lord.

WORDS: JOHN 1:19–23 (BASED ON KING JAMES BIBLE)
MUSIC: ORLANDO GIBBONS (1583–1625)

There are several paintings by the Italian Renaissance painter Raphael (1483–1520) depicting John the Baptist and Jesus together as babies. One of them, known as the *Alba Madonna*, is a round painting (*tondo*), about a metre in diameter, housed in the National Gallery of Art in Washington DC. Recently restored, it is beautiful in every sense of the word, with rich blues, greens and pinks used to depict Mary's clothes, the grass, and the flesh tones of the two children.

In the picture we see Mary humbly seated on the ground against a rural background, reaching out with one hand to steady the two boys, her other hand clasping a Bible, with her finger placed between two pages as if to preserve the page that she is reading. John the Baptist and Jesus are portrayed as though playing together. In John's hand is a little staff, but very clearly at the top we can see a cross-piece, indicating that even at birth there is an overshadowing of the pain and suffering that will emerge when these two little boys are grown up. Although John is holding the little cross up for Jesus, Jesus himself is seen to be grasping it, as though receiving it from his slightly older relative. Nearby, anemones are growing, classically symbolic of Mary's sorrow over the suffering of Christ.

John's cross may be a little one compared to Christ's, but he too will suffer and die, a martyr in the cause of free speech (see Matthew

14:1–13). In another Raphael painting, *The Madonna and Child with the Infant Baptist* (the *Garvagh Madonna*, owned by London's National Gallery), we see the same characters, and a similar staff with a cross. This time, however, it is not the cross that the baby Christ grasps, but a red carnation, symbolizing the pure love that will be expressed by his death. In *The Madonna del Cardellino* (*Madonna of the Goldfinch*, in the Uffizi, Florence), Mary is portrayed reading a book as John hands Jesus a goldfinch, a thistle-eating bird that symbolizes the crown of thorns that Christ will later wear.

It is clear from these pictures and from the Gospels that John and Jesus had an interesting and possibly close relationship. Their mothers were related (Luke 1:36), and Mary visits Elizabeth when pregnant (Luke 1:39–45: see 'Ave Maria', 21 December, p. 114). When Herod eventually kills John in a fit of weakness and false integrity, Jesus is described as withdrawing to a deserted place by himself, presumably to grieve (Matthew 14:13). Luke begins his Gospel with an account of how Zechariah, John's father, is told by the angel Gabriel that in spite of all evidence to the contrary, he and his wife Elizabeth will have a child—a very special, Spirit-filled child who will turn people to God, bringing much joy and preparing the way of the Lord (Luke 1:13–17). Zechariah's response is one of disbelief, which provokes Gabriel to punish him with silence throughout the pregnancy. When eventually John is born, Zechariah is able to speak again. He names the child 'John', as Gabriel instructed him, and then utters a prophecy which is known to the church as the Benedictus, from the Latin for its opening words (Luke 1:68–79).

When Archbishop Thomas Cranmer created the Book of Common Prayer in 1549, he continued the tradition of using Luke 1:68–79 as a canticle, to be said after the second lesson at Morning Prayer every day (except St John the Baptist's Day, 24 June, when it appears within the reading set for the day). Thus Zechariah's prophecy has become part of the spiritual lifeblood of the church: for hundreds of years those at prayer reminded themselves, 'Through the tender mercy of our God, whereby the day-spring from on high hath visited us; to give light to them that sit in darkness, and the shadow of death; and to guide our feet into the way of peace' (Book of Common Prayer). These lines glow with Advent's expectancy of light: during this season we anticipate the blaze of illumination coming into the world with which the other John opens his Gospel (John 1:1–18). He reminds us that his namesake, the Baptist, is not the light, and proceeds immediately to recount the story (told musically by Orlando Gibbons) by which John the Baptist is heard specifically to proclaim the coming of the Messiah and to deny that it is himself.

Orlando Gibbons was one of the greatest English composers of the 17th century, and this setting of a passage from John's Gospel is one of his most famous works. When Gibbons was 21, King James I offered him the post of organist of the Chapel Royal in London, where he remained until his death at the age of 41.

His setting of John 1:19–23 is a distinctive and exquisite piece, which conveys in musical terms the curt and discourteous approach to John by the religious leaders of his day, demanding to know who he is and what is his business. John had been baptizing in the wilderness, and was causing quite a stir by calling sinners to repentence in preparation for the coming of the Messiah (see Matthew 3:1–12). Much of Gibbons' choral music is for unaccompanied choir, but this verse anthem unusually has a contingent of viols (ancestors of the modern violin and viola), to lend weight and add texture to the dramatized account of the encounter. It opens with a few notes on the viols, which are soon joined by a high male voice, narrating the text calmly and gently. The choir respond by singing the words of the priests and Levites, and repeating the story so far told.

Musically speaking, it is antiphonal, with the soloist and choir singing alternately, one answering the other. There are three sections, the first concerning the question 'Who art thou?' which John answers, stating that he is not Christ. The second section has the question 'Art thou Elias?' (Elijah), which John also denies. The third section asks, 'What art thou? that we may give an answer unto them that sent us', in response to which John proclaims himself as the 'voice of him that crieth in the wilderness'. Thus the text lays out a series of questions and answers, and Gibbons' way of structuring his anthem reflects this approach with a question-and-answer style of musical writing. It is a masterly work, so understated in its emotion but powerful in virtue of the simplicity of style, which makes the words clearly understood.

This music is not the equivalent of Renaiassance painting, where almost every brushstroke is loaded with symbolism; rather, Gibbons' approach lets the English text speak clearly, such that we do not need symbols or allegorical images to understand the significance of what is going on. Yet both Raphael and Gibbons have a clear sense of the significance of John as forerunner of Christ, 'making straight' the way of the Lord (Isaiah 40:3), for it is a way that leads through death and resurrection to redemption. And it is the way on which we are all called to walk, whether we live in 16th-century Italy, Elizabethan England or the internet-ready 21st-century global community.

Prayer

Tender, merciful God, who sent your Son Jesus to be the hope of the world, give light to all who sit in darkness and the shadow of death, that all your people may serve you without fear and be guided into the way of peace, which he illuminates this very day. Amen.

THOU WHOSE ALMIGHTY WORD

'Be dressed for action and have your lamps lit; be like those who are waiting for their master to return from the wedding banquet, so that they may open the door for him as soon as he comes and knocks. Blessed are those slaves whom the master finds alert when he comes; truly I tell you, he will fasten his belt and have them sit down to eat, and he will come and serve them. If he comes during the middle of the night, or near dawn, and finds them so, blessed are those slaves.'

LUKE 12:35–38

> *Thou whose almighty word*
> *Chaos and darkness heard,*
> *And took their flight;*
> *Hear us, we humbly pray,*
> *And where the gospel day*
> *Sheds not its glorious ray*
> *Let there be light.*
>
> *Thou who didst come to bring*
> *On thy redeeming wing*
> *Healing and sight,*
> *Health to the sick in mind,*
> *Sight to the inly blind,*
> *O now to all mankind*
> *Let there be light.*

Spirit of truth and love,
Life-giving, holy Dove,
Speed forth thy flight;
Move o'er the waters' face,
Bearing the lamp of grace,
And in earth's darkest place
Let there be light.

Blessed and holy Three,
Glorious Trinity,
Wisdom, Love, Might,
Boundless as ocean's tide
Rolling in fullest pride,
Through the world far and wide
Let there be light.

WORDS: JOHN MARRIOTT (1780–1825)
MUSIC: MOSCOW, ADAPTED FROM FELICE GIARDINI (1716–96)

Advent is a dark time of year in many senses. The Christmas lights may well be up early, but before Christmas Day dawns they serve to emphasize the darkness in which they shine. In the northern hemisphere, the nights are longest at this time of year, and this can affect us in many ways. Some people suffer from a recently recognized condition known as Seasonal Affective Disorder (SAD), which causes a kind of depression brought about by the lack of sunlight. Our bodies and our minds react to, and need, light.

As well as being physically dark, Advent can also be emotionally or spiritually dark. As Christmas approaches, we might be reminded of lost loved ones or of past sadnesses. The lack of light at this time of the year seems to promote reflection on times past and fading memories. In the winter months, some people do not go out at night because they are fearful to walk the streets, and therefore feel more trapped at home at this time of year, as the days are short.

Advent, perhaps more than any other season, can expose brokenness in our lives and world. It is not so much a time to be bleak, but a time to examine the world around us and become aware of the poverty and pain in which so many live. Sometimes it may feel that we have been struck by a ray of darkness, piercing complacency and comfort and destroying security. Even if we reflect on the second coming, we are up against a hope that has so far not materialized. The early church believed in an imminent return of Christ, yet we continue to wait. The master, it seems, has been delayed in his arrival.

It may be helpful to think in terms of a great five-act drama of God that begins with creation, moving into the covenant with the people of Israel (Act Two), followed by the life, death and resurrection of Christ (Act Three). After Christ's resurrection, the fourth act was not then to be his immediate return, but instead the era of the Church, begun by the first disciples and carried on today. One day, we know not when, the curtain will be raised on Act Five, as God gathers up everything in a final blaze of redemptive love and glory. Perhaps our predecessors got their timing wrong, but they had the right idea.

Meanwhile we continue to wait, looking 'through a glass, darkly' (1 Corinthians 13:12, AV). Sometimes that glass is cracked or broken, making it even harder to see or feel well. The experience can be painful: it may be something we see on the television news or more personal, like a family death or break-up, or some crime committed against us. We may feel that in some way God himself is against us. I knew someone once who used to talk of 'the God of the tin hat'. She felt as if God spent most of his time throwing spiritual 'bricks' at her (which is why she needed a tin hat). Her brother, father and fiancé all died in the same year.

Our hope and desire, as Christians, must ultimately be that the light of God will shine in the dark places of sin and despair. We experience this when we place our trust in God and are led away from the darkness of pain to the healing power of Christ's light. It is this desire that prompted John Marriott to write his now-famous hymn. It is thoroughly trinitarian: each of the first three verses takes in turn Father, Son and Holy Spirit, and the fourth is a doxology, praising all three in one. Shining through it is the creative, sustaining and healing light of God. Marriott, ironically, died quite young, of brain disease, and therefore would have experienced the encircling darkness of degenerative illness. A modest man, he would not allow anyone to publish his hymn in his own lifetime. He wrote it with the intention that it be sung to the tune of the British national anthem, but instead it gained a partner in the tune MOSCOW, composed by the Italian operatic composer Felice Giardini (it is known as ITALIAN HYMN in north America). Giardini lived in England for many years, but ended his days in Moscow, the city after which the tune is named. Like Marriott, he knew sadness: he left England when his operas were no longer popular.

It can be very tempting to dwell unduly upon events and feelings that upset us. Nevertheless, comfort is at hand through the ministry of friends and fellow Christians, in whom God's healing Spirit is at work. Through the encounter between light and darkness, sorrow and joy, we may experience an authentic Advent, in which gloom and sorrow are alleviated by a positive hope in the return of Christ to make all things new. Giardini's tune combined with Marriot's words make for a rousing hymn. Singing it in the darkness can help us to remember not only God's light of creation, but also the light of Christ coming into the world, to illuminate, cleanse and heal.

Prayer

O God and Father of all light, look down on your expectant people and give us your hope and your joy, that as we wait upon your promises we may be bathed in the light of your love, until that day when you return in glory to make all things new and good and true in your Son, Jesus Christ our Lord. Amen.

9 December

EARTH WAS WAITING,
SPENT AND RESTLESS

I consider that the sufferings of this present time are not worth comparing with the glory about to be revealed to us. For the creation waits with eager longing for the revealing of the children of God; for the creation was subjected to futility, not of its own will but by the will of the one who subjected it, in hope that the creation itself will be set free from its bondage to decay and will obtain the freedom of the glory of the children of God. We know that the whole creation has been groaning in labour pains until now; and not only the creation, but we ourselves, who have the first fruits of the Spirit, groan inwardly while we wait for adoption, the redemption of our bodies. For in hope we were saved. Now hope that is seen is not hope. For who hopes for what is seen? But if we hope for what we do not see, we wait for it with patience.
ROMANS 8:18–25

Earth was waiting, spent and restless,
with a mingled hope and fear,
faithful men and women praying,
'Surely, Lord, the day is near:
the Desire of all the nations—
it is time he should appear!'

Then the Spirit of the Highest
to a Virgin meek came down,
and he burdened her with blessing,
and he pained her with renown;
for she bore the Lord's Anointed
for his cross and for his crown.

Earth has groaned and laboured for him
since the ages first began,
for in him was hid the secret
which through all the ages ran—
Son of Mary, Son of David,
Son of God, and Son of Man.

WORDS: WALTER CHALMERS SMITH (1824–1908)
MUSIC: PICARDY. FRENCH CAROL FOUND IN TIERSOT'S *MÉLODIES*, PARIS, 1887

Advent is, most of all, a time of waiting—waiting on the Lord, and waiting for the Lord—except that perhaps we have forgotten how to wait. For 21st-century humanity, waiting takes up the space between a desire and a result. We do not want or expect that waiting space to be very big, even though waiting can occupy a significant portion of our lives. Apparently we spend an hour and twelve minutes a week in queues. An hour and twelve minutes seems like a long time to be standing around waiting in our fast-paced society. We have become impatient: we live in the 'now', and have a different sense of time. Our homes are filled with 'labour-saving devices', and the advance of technology is supposed to liberate us from certain activities, giving us more time to do the things we enjoy. This does not always work to our benefit, however, for while we may not have to wash clothes or dishes by hand any more, the burden of loading and unloading machines is a new phenomenon. Computers have given us so many more opportunities both to save time and to fill it up again, as we explore and are frustrated by the amazing things we can (or cannot) do with our fast processors and gigabytes of memory and storage. Time expands to fit things in, perhaps, but many tasks take more time than we expect them to.

All of this can result in constant impatience, frustration with people, machines and other aspects of life that we were once grateful for, but now consider as inconveniences when they don't behave as we want them to. And still we have to wait for things—things we want, things we need and things we dread. We are not in control of our lives as we might want to be, or as we might suppose ourselves to be. We can fly, speak across oceans and access vast amounts of information, but we cannot prevent our deaths, reverse time or predict the future.

The words of this relatively recently written carol reflect today's mood very well. 'Earth was waiting, spent and restless' is a phrase that might apply to an individual, worn out with personal frustrations, or it could apply to the whole world, groaning with exhaustion after a catalogue of natural disasters, shaking, flooding or starving the populations of various corners of the globe. The apostle Paul's references to futility and the bondage of decay are dark words, which seem so apposite when we turn on the television news.

How are we to handle our restlessness, our fear, doubt or despair? So often, our response to frustration or impatience is fatalism: if we cannot control our lives, then we merely accept what is thrown at us, for it is all 'meant to be'. Such an approach is hardly more helpful than the manic desire to control everything and everyone, for fatalism more or less denies us a place in the world, and can lead to a certain abandonment of personal responsibility in actions, relationships or desires. This may well be a problem for our age, in which fatalism and freedom have merged in a society that is both fascinated and appalled by conventional faith.

But Advent is not merely about waiting; it is about hopeful waiting. We wait for our Lord of all hopefulness, praying that the darkness of life today can be illuminated by God's light, burned away in the glow of his love revealed in the redeeming work of Jesus Christ. When we read the passage from Romans carefully, and heed the words of this hymn, we realize that our waiting may not be pleasant. Our purpose on earth in the intervening time is not simply to be entertained in some kind of antechamber to heavenly bliss.

Walter Smith, who wrote 'Earth was restless', was a Scottish minister who, in 1893, was elected Moderator of the Free Church of Scotland. He is perhaps most famous for writing the much-loved hymn 'Immortal, invisible, God only wise':

> Immortal, invisible, God only wise,
> In light inaccessible hid from our eyes,
> Most blessèd, most glorious, the Ancient of Days,
> Almighty, victorious, thy great name we praise.

The last verse of that hymn echoes sentiments that we have already encountered:

> To all life thou givest—to both great and small;
> In all life thou livest, the true life of all;
> We blossom and flourish as leaves on the tree,
> And wither and perish—but nought changeth thee.

It is most unfortunate that the version of 'Immortal, invisible' that is most often sung contains an editorial amendment, which cuts out the only reference to Christ in the hymn. To some, therefore, Smith is a writer of a hymn that does not mention Jesus. Originally, 'Immortal invisible' concluded with the lines 'And so let thy glory, almighty, impart, through Christ in his story, thy Christ to the heart'. We see the same approach in 'Earth was waiting':

> For in him was hid the secret
> which through all the ages ran—
> Son of Mary, Son of David,
> Son of God, and Son of Man.

For Smith, the solution to doom and gloom is to be found in Christ, the immortal, invisible light, supremely human, supremely divine, through whom the redemption of the whole creation becomes possible.

The old French tune PICARDY, which fits so well with Smith's words, is more often associated with the ancient hymn 'Let all mortal flesh keep silence'. That eucharistic hymn has a seasonal flavour too, and the sense of reverence conveyed by a slow rendition of the tune can equally reflect the mysteriousness of the incarnation. For Smith's Advent hymn, the impact of the tune is equally powerful, yet different. His text has a melancholic feel in places, and the sombreness of the tune can echo it. Alternatively, this dignified tune can feel almost aggressive or agitated if played quite fast, and some people might feel that it suits Smith's text better that way. Thus, the hymn can truly reflect our mood. For some, the thought of an end time when creation's groaning will cease and Christ will return is something rather terrifying, while for others it is something eagerly anticipated, to be greeted as joyfully as the first incarnation 2000 years ago. The thought of the glory of God revealed in a second coming of Christ is truly an amazing one, which we can hardly comprehend, although it may not be so hard to welcome the idea that the pain of the world can be likened to labour pains, excruciating to bear but necessary for a wonderful, exciting and new creation.

Prayer

O Jesus, Son of Mary, Son of David, bless us when we feel burdened with the cares of the world or pained by the hurts of others, that we may be refreshed by the mystery of your presence among us, and inspired by the renown of your cross-crowning love, for you are Son of God, and Son of Man, then, now and for ever. Amen.

PEOPLE, LOOK EAST

Arise, shine; for your light has come, and the glory of the Lord has risen upon you. For darkness shall cover the earth, and thick darkness the peoples; but the Lord will arise upon you, and his glory will appear over you. Nations shall come to your light, and kings to the brightness of your dawn. Lift up your eyes and look around; they all gather together, they come to you; your sons shall come from far away, and your daughters shall be carried on their nurses' arms. Then you shall see and be radiant; your heart shall thrill and rejoice, because the abundance of the sea shall be brought to you, the wealth of the nations shall come to you.
ISAIAH 60:1–5

People, look East, the time is near
of the crowning of the year.
Make your house fair as you are able,
trim the hearth, and set the table.
People, look East, and sing today:
Love the Guest is on the way.

Furrows, be glad, though earth is bare,
one more seed is planted there:
Give up your strength the seed to nourish,
that in course the flower may flourish.
People, look East, and sing today:
Love the Rose is on the way.

Stars, keep the watch, when night is dim
one more light the bowl shall brim.
Shining beyond the frosty weather,
bright as sun and moon together.
People, look East, and sing today:
Love the Star is on the way.

Angels, announce to man and beast
Him who cometh from the East.
Set ev'ry peak and valley humming
with the word, the Lord is coming.
People, look East, and sing today:
Love the Lord is on the way.

WORDS: ELEANOR FARJEON (1881–1965) © OXFORD UNIVERSITY PRESS.
MUSIC: 17TH CENTURY OR EARLIER, FROM A FRENCH BESANÇON MANUSCRIPT,
'CHANTONS, BARGIÉS, NOUÉ, NOUÉ'

The English writer Eleanor Farjeon may be best remembered as the author of the hymn 'Morning has broken', but she also wrote collections of stories, three plays based on fairy tales, 33 collections of poetry, and eight other books. She also wrote eleven novels, as well as plays, poetry and biographical works, and she was a friend of D.H. Lawrence and Walter de la Mare.

Her Advent carol, 'People, look East', draws its title from a passage in the book of Baruch:

Arise, O Jerusalem, stand upon the height; look toward the east, and see your children gathered from west and east at the word of the Holy One, rejoicing that God has remembered them. For they went out from you on foot, led away by their enemies; but God will bring them back to you, carried in glory, as on a royal throne.
BARUCH 5:5–7

Baruch was Jeremiah's secretary (see Jeremiah 32:12–16), but it is unlikely that he actually wrote the book which bears his name, and which is not officially a part of the Bible. Nevertheless, Baruch is written from the perspective of dispersed Jews, and contains a wonderful passage that looks both forward and eastward to salvation. Baruch's readers are literally looking eastward to Jerusalem, their homeland, from which they have been exiled. Nowadays we might recall that the sun rises in the east, and thus it is in that direction that we look for the rising of Christ—the advent of the sun of righteousness. Isaiah writes in a similar vein in that most evocative passage, 'Arise, shine; for your light has come.' He also tells his people to look eastward to the rising of the sun, and proclaims a time when those far away will return at the dawn of a new age of prosperity and joy, replacing the sufferings of exile.

Eleanor Farjeon's spiritual journey was a long one, which culminated with her becoming a Roman Catholic at the age of 70. 'People, look East' was one of six carols that she wrote for her friend Percy Dearmer's groundbreaking *The Oxford Book of Carols*, published in 1928. The words are striking, and are reminiscent of the Benedicite, a canticle which is often substituted for the Te Deum at Morning Prayer during Advent and Lent. (A canticle is a biblical text or collection of verses arranged for singing or chanting.) Its text comes from the 'Song of the Three', which is the apocryphal prayer of thanksgiving offered by Shadrach, Meshach and Abednego when they remained unhurt upon being cast into the fiery furnace for refusing to worship King Nebuchadnezzar's golden statue. In it we find these verses:

Bless the Lord, ye fire and heat; cold and chill, bless ye the Lord. Bless the Lord, dews and hoar frosts; frost and cold, bless the Lord. Bless the Lord, ice and snow; nights and days, bless the Lord... Bless the Lord, ye mountains and hills; everything growing from the earth, bless the Lord.
BOOK OF COMMON PRAYER

There is a similar 'earthy' theme in Farjeon's words, which seem to combine the feel of winter 'good cheer' with a biblical resonance and theological purpose. This theology is expressed in the last line of each verse: 'Love', personified in Christ, is the guest, the rose, the star and the Lord. In this imagery we are reminded that Christ comes among us, as one of us but also as a kind of stranger, a guest, whom we must welcome—and we must prepare to welcome him into our homes and our hearts. The idea of 'Christ the rose' is derived from a reference in Song of Songs 2:1: 'I am a rose of Sharon, a lily of the valleys.' Unfortunately, the Hebrew word is best translated as 'crocus', but it provides the background to the idea that Christ is like a rose. Sharon is where David's cattle were grazed (1 Chronicles 27:29). The Sharon rose is quite large, growing up to twelve feet tall, with pink, blue, purple or white flowers.

The jaunty tune goes at a fair lick, sometimes catching singers out, but the hurried excitement that it expresses is highly appropriate for this 'Carol of the Advent', as it is subtitled. As we venture further into Advent, Christmas draws ever closer. Advent is, strictly speaking, a time when we prepare for the second coming of Christ, but we can hardly escape the necessary preparations for Christmas too. Farjeon's idea of 'trimming the hearth' and making the house ready is very apt, for time is certainly running out! Sending Christmas cards becomes something of a priority at around this time, and while a great deal of effort, expense and time is involved, it is lovely to send and receive them.

Christmas cards make very good decorations, brightening up the home and giving a distinctive flavour to December décor. More importantly, other people provide them. At this time of year we allow others to adorn our living and work spaces with whatever *they* want. No matter how gaudy their goodwill is, we pin it up, welcoming friends, family and acquaintances as guests of love into our homes.

Obviously, many seasonal cards are not really about Christmas at all. Rudolf, sleigh rides and the snowman all make their inevitable appearance. But some cards are Christian, and actually contain messages about Jesus and why Christmas is important. Writing Christmas cards can be like a form of prayer. As we write a greeting and perhaps a little news on each one, we may find ourselves praying for the recipient. Some people only really 'exist' for us in the sense that they are on that Christmas card list, but each year we exchange greetings. They may be on the fringe of our lives, but we do care about them. Not all prayer is conducted on our knees: some can be done with a pen and address book during Advent.

When we exchange Christmas cards, we get in touch with people from our past lives, people who have moved away, or from whom we have moved away. Christmas is a time for catching up, even if it does mean reading and writing circular letters of diverse length and appeal. Christmas is a time for news—good news mostly. Unfortunately, though, we sometimes have to receive or send sad news in the annual Christmas card, and that is one of the reasons why December can bring sorrow as well as joy. Some people try to immerse themselves in the commercial joy of Christmas as a form of escapism, only to find that their tinselled happiness goes hollow because they are grieving below the surface. Even if this is so, they may be greatly comforted by a card received from someone who really cares and takes the trouble and effort to write a truly personal greeting which conveys hope, prayer and love. Thus there can still be 'good news' for those who are sad at this time of year.

In all this 'catching up' with friends, we also 'catch up' with ourselves, and with God. The Christmas season falls at the end of the year, when we tend to look over our shoulders at the past, perhaps selecting the best and worst morsels. Christmas cards help us with this: through cards received and sent, we re-enter periods of joy and pain that shaped us, and we delve into distant memories. Such reflection can be good for us, leading us on to reflect on other things—the passage of time, our relationship with God, our past, and our hopes for the future.

The first Christmas cards were sent by Henry Cole in 1843, who, when he found that he hadn't time to write to his acquaintances, employed an artist to design a card. In 2003, two billion Christmas cards were sent in the UK and a similar amount in the USA, and there's no reason to suppose that there will be any fewer this year. These cards, whether those who give and receive them know it or not, speak of cares and prayers, caught in thoughts of love for others.

And that, on one level, is what Christmas is all about—in which case, it is and will always be good news, not only from the east, but from all points west, north and south.

Prayer

Father God, you greet us in Christ by his birth among us, and by your Holy Spirit you continue to offer your saving love to every corner of the world. As we send seasonal greetings to those whom we love and care for, hear the unspoken prayers of our hearts, and bless all those to whom we write, whether they be near or far. Amen.

BORN IN THE NIGHT

And he will come to Zion as Redeemer, to those in Jacob who turn from transgression, says the Lord. And as for me, this is my covenant with them, says the Lord: my spirit that is upon you, and my words that I have put in your mouth, shall not depart out of your mouth, or out of the mouths of your children, or out of the mouths of your children's children, says the Lord, from now on and forever.

Arise, shine; for your light has come, and the glory of the Lord has risen upon you. For darkness shall cover the earth, and thick darkness the peoples; but the Lord will arise upon you, and his glory will appear over you. Nations shall come to your light, and kings to the brightness of your dawn. Lift up your eyes and look around; they all gather together, they come to you; your sons shall come from far away, and your daughters shall be carried on their nurses' arms. Then you shall see and be radiant; your heart shall thrill and rejoice, because the abundance of the sea shall be brought to you, the wealth of the nations shall come to you.

ISAIAH 59:20—60:5

Born in the night,
  Mary's child.
A long way from your home;
Coming in need,
  Mary's child,
Born in a borrowed room.

Clear shining light,
  Mary's child,
Your face lights up our way;
Light of the world,
  Mary's child,
Dawn on our darkened day.

Truth of our life,
  Mary's child,
You tell us God is good;
Prove it is true,
  Mary's child,
Go to your cross of wood.

Hope of the world,
  Mary's child,
You're coming soon to reign;
King of the earth,
  Mary's child,
Walk in our streets again.

WORDS AND MUSIC: GEOFFREY AINGER (B. 1925) © STAINER AND BELL

Among the hundreds of Advent and Christmas carols that are available to us to sing, meditate upon, pray through and worship with, this one is distinctive because it is addressed *to* Jesus. Very few of the carols that English-speakers love to sing are actually addressed to Jesus, or even to God, although there are the more sentimental kind, addressed as rocking carols to an idealized baby Jesus, as in 'The rocking carol' and the second half of 'Away in a manger':

> *... I love thee, Lord Jesus! Look down from the sky,*
> *And stay by my bedside till morning is nigh.*

Be near me, Lord Jesus; I ask thee to stay
Close by me for ever, and love me, I pray.
Bless all the dear children in thy tender care,
And fit us for heaven, to live with thee there.

Other hymns, such as 'As with gladness, men of old' and Graham Kendrick's 'The Servant King' do contain one verse each addressed to Jesus, but they are mostly in the third person singular, rather than addressing Christ directly. The final verse of 'O come, all ye faithful' turns in a similar direction for its special final verse: 'Yea, Lord, we greet thee, born this happy morning'. I mention these because they are notable rarities, and it is striking how few carols address Jesus at all, even in passing.

Meanwhile, we are happy to address ourselves and each other in most of the hymns and carols we sing. Many are a rallying cry to offer praise, to 'come and worship', and they often do this by re-telling the story of the incarnation. Some carols—strangely, perhaps —are addressed to slaughtered children ('The Coventry Carol'); to the Christmas tree ('O Tannenbaum'); to Mary ('Mary, blessed teenage mother'); to Jesus' birthplace ('Bethlehem of noblest cities' and 'O little town of Bethlehem') or to angels ('Angels from the realms of glory'). Other carols are narrative, even dramatic in form ('Good King Wenceslas' and 'We three kings').

With 'Born in the night', however, we can rejoice in a set of words that unashamedly form a prayer to Jesus. And what a lovely carol this is: the words are powerful, and the tune (MARY'S CHILD) is delightful. Put together, they contrast profoundly, for words and music bring out and emphasize the joy and the pain which spell out the irony of Christmas. Here in words and music is a carol that warms our hearts with the good news, sounding a bit like a lilting lullaby, but which also cuts us to the quick with its honesty about the circumstances of Christ's birth, the darkness of the world, the crucifixion and the second coming.

At first glance, it may appear that Geoffrey Ainger is telling us that Jesus was born in the middle of the night. Many people believe that he was, of course: the angels appear to the shepherds by night, and the wise men follow a star, all of which lures us into the Christmas card image of a night-time birth in a nice clean stable, under a clear midnight sky. Perhaps Mary was in labour for part of a night (many mothers are!), but this romanticized vision is not directly drawn from scripture, and we might even note that the shepherds were told that 'this day' a child has been born (Luke 2:11). The 'night' of the carol is not simply a reference to the popular assumption that Jesus was born in the hours of darkness, but it is a metaphorical night: the night-time of the world, a dark time in which Christ, light of the world, appears. We may not be sure of the literal truth of Christ's being 'born in the night', but references to the 'cross of wood' remind us of its truth in spiritual terms. Christ came, as in the words of Isaiah's prophecy, to a people who 'walked in darkness' (Isaiah 9:2).

There are ambiguities in the carol too. In the first verse there is a reference to 'coming in need', and this could signal the helplessness of Jesus the baby, needing Mary, needing shelter and his parents' love, acceptance and care; or it could be a reference to the world in need of a Saviour. There are resonances in this carol which cause us to think of those who are homeless, of those who feel that they need some kind of proof of faith before committing themselves to Christ, and of those who long to see the coming of God's kingdom. The phrase 'walk in our streets again', with which the carol so movingly closes, is an ambiguous one, open to interpretation. It could be taken as a reference to a bodily return of Christ, of his 'being seen among us' once again, or it could be interpreted as an acknowledgment that Christ walks among us by his Spirit, walking in our streets wherever there is need, suffering or darkness. We find hope in the conclusion of this carol—the hope of the world, the hoped-for return of Christ, which forms the theme of Advent.

Geoffrey Ainger, the British author of this moving prayer-carol, was a Methodist minister and wrote 'Born in the night' when he was based in his home county of Essex between 1958 and 1962. Then he moved to Notting Hill in west London, and in 1964 a collection entitled *Songs from Notting Hill* was published, in which the carol first appeared. The small volume contained eight songs in total, the words to six of which were by Geoffrey Ainger (four of them also had tunes by him). The Notting Hill Music Group, who compiled the booklet, said of it that they had done it for themselves: these were songs that they had written and enjoyed, through which they expressed themselves in worship, satire, doubt or even resentment, where appropriate. They hoped to promote a form of worship music that would be equally at home in or out of churches, drawing on the folk music origins of much hymnody, and especially carols. Their intention in publishing 'Born in the night' and other songs was to provoke either an acceptance of their approach or a sense of exasperation that would encourage others to try to do better!

The spirit of this approach pervades 'Born in the night', for there is both gentle desire and melodic pleasantry in the words and music, but also a sting in the tail of each verse. This is not a carol that allows us to hide from the meaning, impact or significance of Christmas, and for that it must be welcomed and should be better known.

Prayer

Mary's child Jesus, hope of the world, light up the way of faith for all who walk in doubt, loneliness, need or darkness. As you are goodness and truth in human form, grant us to borrow from you some splinters of your compassion, that in our small way we may anticipate the coming of your kingdom here on this fragile earth, for you are coming to reign, in the name of the Father and in the power of the Spirit. Amen.

THE LAMB

The next day he saw Jesus coming towards him and declared, 'Here is the Lamb of God who takes away the sin of the world! This is he of whom I said, "After me comes a man who ranks ahead of me because he was before me." I myself did not know him; but I came baptizing with water for this reason, that he might be revealed to Israel.' And John testified, 'I saw the Spirit descending from heaven like a dove, and it remained on him. I myself did not know him, but the one who sent me to baptize with water said to me, "He on whom you see the Spirit descend and remain is the one who baptizes with the Holy Spirit." And I myself have seen and have testified that this is the Son of God.' The next day John again was standing with two of his disciples, and as he watched Jesus walk by, he exclaimed, 'Look, here is the Lamb of God!' The two disciples heard him say this, and they followed Jesus.

JOHN 1:29–37

Little Lamb, who made thee?
Dost thou know who made thee?
Gave thee life, and bid thee feed
By the stream and o'er the mead;
Gave thee clothing of delight,
Softest clothing, woolly, bright;
Gave thee such a tender voice,
Making all the vales rejoice?
Little Lamb, who made thee?
Dost thou know who made thee?

Little Lamb, I'll tell thee,
Little Lamb, I'll tell thee:
He is called by thy name,
For he calls himself a Lamb.
He is meek, and he is mild;
He became a little child.
I a child, and thou a lamb.
We are called by his name.
Little Lamb, God bless thee!
Little Lamb, God bless thee!

WORDS: WILLIAM BLAKE (1757–1827)
MUSIC: JOHN TAVENER (B. 1934)

The significance of sheep is well attested in the Bible. According to my computer, there are 189 references to sheep in the New Revised Standard Version of the Bible, and if you add in words like 'ewe' and 'ram', you get over 700 references. Adam's son Abel kept sheep (Genesis 4:2), and they were probably the indigenous breed to the area, *ovis orientalis* (eastern sheep), sometimes called broad-tailed sheep. Their wool kept people warm, while the horns could be used for holding fluids (see 1 Samuel 16:1) or as musical instruments, and were used to devastating effect at the battle of Jericho (Joshua 6:1–20). The milk was drunk or curdled, and the meat was eaten or offered in sacrifice to God—and that broad tail was often reserved for this ritual purpose (see Exodus 29:22–25).

The most important biblical story about roast lamb is, of course, the one that precedes the final flight from Egypt, when the angel of death 'passes over' the Israelites, striking down the firstborn of the Egyptians. The people of God are instructed to kill a lamb, smear its blood on the doorway as a sign of allegiance to God, and to eat the flesh, hastily, in readiness for flight (Exodus 12). The Passover is a continuing memorial of that ancient and significant event.

Sheep were incredibly useful animals and were easily domesticated. As such they were immensely valuable (2 Kings 3:4) and had to be looked after and guarded. King David, we know, was not only a good musician and giant killer, but he started his career as a shepherd, keeping predators away from the flock at night (see Amos 3:12). The shepherds in the story of Jesus' birth were doing much the same (Luke 2:8–20). At night, the shepherd would bring the animals safely into a cave or some other fold, and would sleep across the entrance to protect them, literally 'laying down his life' for them (John 10:1–18).

By the time we reach the Gospels, we have stories of lost sheep and a good shepherd, but also the famous statement from John the Baptist, who identifies Jesus as the Lamb of God (John 1:36). New Testament theology associates Jesus with that first lamb of God, the Passover lamb of Exodus 12, and in John's Gospel the crucifixion is described as taking place while the Passover lambs were being slaughtered in readiness for the festival the following day (John 19:14–16). Easter and Passover are inextricably and symbolically linked, as are Passover and eucharist.

But Jesus is not only associated with the sacrificial lamb, whose blood is spilt so that his people may be saved. Jesus is also the good shepherd, the carer, the shepherd of our souls (see 1 Peter 2:25). The prophet Ezekiel foresaw this when he wrote, 'For thus says the Lord God: I myself will search for my sheep, and will seek them out. As shepherds seek out their flocks when they are among their scattered sheep, so I will seek out my sheep' (Ezekiel 34:11–12).

Here is Christ the pastor, the model for Christian ministry. The ordination service in the Church of England calls on all clergy to remember to 'set the Good Shepherd always before (you) as the pattern of his calling', and to 'Remember always with thanksgiving that the treasure now to be entrusted to you is Christ's own flock, bought through the shedding of his blood on the cross.' Bishops are told to 'keep watch over the whole flock in which the Holy Spirit has appointed you shepherd'.

The blending of sheep and shepherd comes together in the book of Revelation, when we read that Christ is both shepherd and lamb, 'for the Lamb at the centre of the throne will be their shepherd, and he will guide them to springs of the water of life, and God will wipe away every tear from their eyes' (Revelation 7:17).

William Blake played on this overlap of sheep and shepherd in his delightful children's poem, 'The Lamb', which was part of his collection *Songs of Innocence*, written in 1789. He added *Songs of Experience* in 1794, creating a double set of poetry that underlined the tragic but truthful discrepancy in life between the world of pastoral innocence and the cynical, repressed world of adulthood. So we have the apparent meekness of 'The Lamb', which contrasts with 'The Tyger' in *Songs of Experience* ('Tyger, tyger, burning bright! ... did he who made the lamb, make thee?)

Both these poems have been set to music by the contemporary composer John Tavener, and 'The Lamb', composed in 1982, has become a favourite for unaccompanied choir. It is quite a simple piece, but contains within itself a harmonic ambiguity, which becomes apparent when semitones clash on the words 'clothing of delight'. It begs the question, is it in a major or a minor key? The answer appears to be, a bit of both. We are transported to Blake's innocent world of childhood, but as the music drifts in its haunting way, we are never quite allowed to become submerged in a safe soundworld. There are melancholic undertones which speak of the tragedy of lost innocence, of the fact that the little lamb will not live long; that the cute animal beloved of little children has the same creator as you and I. It is an unusual Christmas carol and, like most, is popular because it sounds nice and has sentimental words. But listen to the music carefully and study the words, and there is darkness within—the darkness of future pain and of betrayal. The innocence of the Christ-child will be betrayed and the roles reversed as we become the children, the children of God, and Jesus the lamb, sacrificed once and for all upon the cross.

Prayer

Salvation belongs to you, our God who is seated on the throne, and to the Lamb! As we remember that your Son was born innocent of all sin, but chose to taint himself with the sin of the world, help us always to praise you: blessing and glory and wisdom and thanksgiving and honour and power and might be to you for ever and ever! Amen.

SANTA LUCIA

'You are the light of the world. A city built on a hill cannot be hidden. No one after lighting a lamp puts it under the bushel basket, but on the lampstand, and it gives light to all in the house. In the same way, let your light shine before others, so that they may see your good works and give glory to your Father in heaven.'
MATTHEW 5:14–16

Hark! through the darksome night
Sounds come a winging:
Lo! 'tis the Queen of Light
Joyfully singing.
Clad in her garment white,
Wearing her crown of light,
Santa Lucia, Santa Lucia.

Deep in the northern sky
Bright stars are beaming;
Christmas is drawing nigh,
Candles are gleaming.
Welcome you vision rare,
Lights glowing in your hair.
Santa Lucia, Santa Lucia.

The darkness shall soon depart
from the earth's valleys
thus she speaks
a wonderful word to us

The day shall rise anew
from the rosy sky.
Santa Lucia, Santa Lucia.

WORDS AND MUSIC: TRADITIONAL (TRANSLATION COMPILED FROM VARIOUS SOURCES

Today is the feast day of St Lucy, patron saint of the blind. According to various legends and sources, she was martyred in 304 in Syracuse, Sicily. She is still revered as the patron saint of that city (although her body is now said to lie in Venice), and she is associated with light because it was said that she used to visit Christians who were in hiding in dark underground tunnels. To light the way she wore a wreath of candles on her head.

Apparently her family was wealthy, but her father died young, leaving her in the care of her widowed mother, who intended her to marry a pagan called Paschiasus. Lucy preferred to remain unmarried and went to pray at the tomb of St Agatha, which was in Catania, also in Sicily. Consequently, her mother was cured of a long illness, and became more amenable to her daughter's request not to marry but instead to give her wealth to the poor and commit her life to God. Her suitor was less impressed, though, and denounced her to the Roman authorities. They determined that she should be sent to a brothel, but Lucy refused and they could not enforce the ruling. According to legend, she plucked out her own eyes and sent them to Paschiasus on a plate, which is why she is often portrayed in art as carrying a dish containing her eyes. (Other legends say that her eyes were put out by her persecutors.) Then she was condemned to be burnt alive, but she proved to be impervious to the flames, so she was finally killed by the sword.

All this is likely to have taken place during the reign of Emperor Diocletian (284–305), who instigated a particularly severe persecution in 303. By the eighth century, Lucy's fame had spread to Britain, where two early churches are known to be dedicated to her.

Nowadays, Lucy is largely forgotten in Britain, but she is still revered in Scandinavia. For this day, each village elects its own Lucia (or Lucy), and this 'Lucia Queen', wearing a crown of lit candles, leads children singing traditional carols in a procession through the home or in the streets. In Stockholm each year, the 'Lucia Queen' is crowned by the winner of the Nobel Prize for Literature. Lucia's Day symbolically opens the Christmas celebrations in Scandinavia, bringing hope and light during the darkest months of the year, for far into the northern hemisphere there are days with no sunlight at all for part of the year. Before the reform of the Gregorian calendar in the 16th century, Lucy's Day fell on the winter solstice (now December 21), the shortest day. The English poet and cleric, John Donne, reminds us of this in his poem, 'A Nocturnal Upon St Lucy's Day, Being The Shortest Day'.

Scandinavia became Christian around AD1000, and as the winter solstice festival fell on the same day as St Lucy's Day, both pagan and Christian traditions mixed to become the modern Lucia celebration. Stories of her courage had been taken to Sweden by missionaries and she became known as the 'Lucia Bride', or 'Lucia Queen'. It was said that, wearing white robes and a crown of light, she would deliver food and drink to the poor, and the idea grew that on her feast day she would lead the way for the sun to bring longer days. 'St Lucy's fires' were lit in the evening and incense was thrown into the flames. People danced in the smoke, believing that it would protect them from witchcraft and disease.

This blend of Christian legend and pagan ritual has become a very significant festival in Scandinavian tradition. The feast of St Lucy ('Santa Lucia') is now celebrated as a festival of light, and it has spread to churches all over the world, including St Paul's Cathedral in London, where Santa Lucia is celebrated with a blend of Christmas carols, processions, preaching and pagan ritual. At the heart of the service is the Santa Lucia procession, headed by a girl wearing a crown of candles and escorted by other young people as she brings in the light. All are dressed in white, bearing candles and singing, and the boys wear traditional white cone-shaped hats. We might think of Christ, the light of the world, born in a dark stable to bring light and life, or we might think of the ancient festivals of light that marked the turning of the globe, hailing the beginning of the end of the long nights, and the return of the sun.

The music for the Santa Lucia, ironically, has nothing to do with Scandinavia, but consists of a Latin text set to a very simple, haunting melody. The tune is like a lullaby, and is repeated many times during the procession. Every year the Santa Lucia procession never fails to move the congregation, as a youthful, beautiful choir enter a dark church, bringing with them a celebration of light, life and hope.

The beautiful Santa Lucia festival reminds us that there are many ways to celebrate the hopes of Advent and the joys of Christmas. People are serving Christ in ways of which we cannot conceive, worshipping God in ways that have drawn on their unique culture, history and identity. We might be tempted to be suspicious of the association of St Lucy with Christmas and the welcoming of the light, but it is better to see the value, the beauty and devotion that accompany what otherwise might be considered strange. Nowadays it seems that St Lucy's Christian roots are once again at the heart of the festival, for while there are pagan overtones to a festival of light, the Scandinavian churches have thoroughly adopted the festival, and would always seek to remind us that while 'Lucy' might mean 'light', the light which she brings, and which burns in all those candles on her head, is none other than the light of Christ, shining in this dark world of sin.

Prayer

O Lord, the light of whose love shines in the world, accept our praises and prayers, that, illuminated by you, we may always offer worship worthy of your glory, until that day when we, with all who are clothed in white, shall sit at your feet in the heavenly kingdom, where you reign, king of light and truth, with the Father and Holy Spirit, ever one God, now and for ever. Amen.

OF THE FATHER'S HEART
BEGOTTEN

An account of the genealogy of Jesus the Messiah, the son of David, the son of Abraham. Abraham was the father of Isaac, and Isaac the father of Jacob, and Jacob the father of Judah and his brothers, and Judah the father of Perez and Zerah by Tamar, and Perez the father of Hezron, and Hezron the father of Aram, and Aram the father of Aminadab, and Aminadab the father of Nahshon, and Nahshon the father of Salmon, and Salmon the father of Boaz by Rahab, and Boaz the father of Obed by Ruth, and Obed the father of Jesse, and Jesse the father of King David.

And David was the father of Solomon by the wife of Uriah, and Solomon the father of Rehoboam, and Rehoboam the father of Abijah, and Abijah the father of Asaph, and Asaph the father of Jehoshaphat, and Jehoshaphat the father of Joram, and Joram the father of Uzziah, and Uzziah the father of Jotham, and Jotham the father of Ahaz, and Ahaz the father of Hezekiah, and Hezekiah the father of Manasseh, and Manasseh the father of Amos, and Amos the father of Josiah, and Josiah the father of Jechoniah and his brothers, at the time of the deportation to Babylon.

And after the deportation to Babylon: Jechoniah was the father of Salathiel, and Salathiel the father of Zerubbabel, and Zerubbabel the father of Abiud, and Abiud the father of Eliakim, and Eliakim the father of Azor, and Azor the father of Zadok, and Zadok the father of Achim, and Achim the father of Eliud, and Eliud the father of Eleazar, and Eleazar the father of Matthan, and Matthan the father of Jacob, and Jacob the father of Joseph the husband of Mary, of whom Jesus was born, who is called the Messiah.

So all the generations from Abraham to David are fourteen generations; and from David to the deportation to Babylon, fourteen generations; and from the deportation to Babylon to the Messiah, fourteen generations.

MATTHEW 1:1–17

Of the Father's heart begotten,
Ere the world from chaos rose,
He is Alpha: from that Fountain
All that is and hath been flows;
He is Omega, of all things
Yet to come the mystic Close,
Evermore and evermore.

O how blest that wondrous birthday,
When the Maid the curse retrieved,
Brought to birth mankind's salvation,
By the Holy Ghost conceived;
And the Babe, the world's Redeemer,
In her loving arms received,
Evermore and evermore.

This is he, whom seer and sybil
Sang in ages long gone by;
This is he of old revealed
In the page of prophecy;
Lo! he comes the promised Saviour;
Let the world his praises cry!
Evermore and evermore.

Let the storm and summer sunshine,
Gliding stream and sounding shore,
Sea and forest, frost and zephyr,
Day and night their Lord adore;
Let creation join to laud thee
Through the ages evermore,
Evermore and evermore.

Sing, ye heights of heaven, his praises;
Angels and Archangels, sing!
Wheresoe'er ye be, ye faithful,
Let your joyous anthems ring,
Every tongue his name confessing,
Countless voices answering
Evermore and evermore.

WORDS: LATIN, BY PRUDENTIUS, TRANS. ROBY FURLEY DAVIS (1866–1937)
MUSIC: *DIVINUM MYSTERIUM*. MELODY FROM *PIAE CANTIONES*,
THEODERICI PETRI NYLANDENSIS, 1582

At the very beginning of Matthew's Gospel we find what the NRSV calls 'the genealogy of Jesus the Messiah'. Matthew wants to remind us that Jesus had a significant birth-line, through Joseph, the husband of his mother. It seems like just a list of names, and is often ignored. But in these names, some obscure, some familiar, we see people whose role in the history of salvation was immensely significant, and others who are hardly remembered today. Matthew's list is a golden thread of spiritual greatness, sewing together the greatest lineage ever recorded. He knew his heritage well, and, in writing for those who had a sense of their place in history, he draws Jesus' family tree in great detail. His readers knew these figures better than we do now, and would have been suitably impressed by the connections he makes. That Jesus was directly descended from Abraham and David was of great importance to the Jews whom Matthew was evangelizing.

It is not only about *who* you know, but *what* you know. In that thread lie strands of wisdom, passed from one generation to another. Just as musicians like to trace their musical education back to a great composer or virtuoso, religious leaders sometimes boast of their mentors, having learnt from widely respected elders. Jesus, therefore, is presented as sitting at the feet of a revered line of religious leaders. So it is not just who his earthly ancestors were that matters, but the fact that they were also his spiritual fathers. For then it adds up and points us towards a recognition of who his heavenly Father was, and is, and ever shall be.

We should not be surprised that there is sin in this list. There is sin everywhere, even among those whom we revere as great religious leaders. This may be a list of spiritual heroes, with whom Matthew wants to associate Jesus, but as saints they are also sinners. David, infamously, committed adultery with Bathsheba, the wife of Uriah the Hittite, whom David caused to be killed in battle (see 2 Samuel 11); and his son Solomon, although blessed with wisdom, was not without his faults (see 1 Kings 11). Solomon's son Rehoboam also forsook the law of the Lord (2 Chronicles 12:1). So it continues, until we reach the man at the head of the list: Jesus. The others, like every human being before or since, were weak and committed sin. Matthew's genealogy carries us through sin until we reach Jesus, who, because he himself is divine and sinless, clears sin away by his death, and turns us all around, pointing us in a new direction and sending us on our way along the road to salvation.

We can see in this list not only a sense of Jesus' place in history, but a sense of the pace of history. Forty-two generations are listed, and Matthew suggests that it was not really very long between Abraham and Christ. Thus Abraham is made real to Jesus' generation, while we need only go back 33 60-year lifetimes to meet Christ. Seen like this, the events of the Bible seem much closer than we might have realized. By reminding his readers of the relatively recent history preceding the birth of Christ, Matthew brings this world nearer in time, and as we read it now, we are reminded that we are closer in time to Matthew than he was to Abraham.

There is, of course, a longer and deeper dimension, which is referred to in the great Latin Christmas hymn, 'Of the Father's heart begotten'. To some it is known as 'Of the Father's love begotten', but 'heart' seems better as a direct translation of the Latin *corde* found in the original fourth-century text, which is derived from a 37-verse poem entitled 'Hymn for every hour' by Marcus Aurelius Clemens Prudentius, a Spanish lawyer who retired at the age of 57 to write poetry and hymns. 'Of the Father's heart' was adopted in the ninth century by the Spanish church as a liturgical hymn for use around 1 January (the Feast of the Circumcision, or Naming of Jesus). The refrain 'Evermore and evermore' did not appear for another couple of centuries. There have been various translations into English, the most recent and most effective being the nine-verse one by R.F. Davis which he made for the *English Hymnal* (1906). Seven of these verses found their way into *The New English Hymnal* (1980), and the most popular are printed here.

The tune that is invariably used has slightly obscure origins in medieval eucharistic liturgy, being first found in eleventh- and twelfth-century documents from Italy and Germany. It was John Mason Neale and Thomas Helmore who took it from the Finnish musical collection *Piae Cantiones* (1582). Other well-known carols derived from this collection are '*In dulci jubilo*' and 'Good King Wenceslas' (see 26 December, p. 141). The coupling of words and tune has been largely successful: both have an ancient feel, carrying us on a wave of narrative that reminds us of the great sweep of time and purpose that the incarnation encompasses. It begins with references to Jesus as Alpha and Omega (see Revelation 1:8; 21:6; 22:13), which is also hinted at in Colossians 1:15–20: the Christ who was before all things and in all things. Matthew may have a human genealogy to show us at the beginning of his Gospel, but God himself has a whole eternity stretching before and after, from which to reveal his loving self in his only begotten Son.

Prayer

Creator God, Father of Jesus from before the world began, your mercy beams from on high like summer sunshine in the dark winter of our hearts. Take the imperfections of our lives and turn them to good, so that we, with all the generations of your children who have gone before us, may find your name on our lips and your love in our hearts, for you reign, Father, Son and Holy Spirit, evermore and evermore. Amen.

THIS IS THE TRUTH
SENT FROM ABOVE

Then the Lord God formed man from the dust of the ground, and breathed into his nostrils the breath of life; and the man became a living being... The Lord God took the man and put him in the garden of Eden to till it and keep it. And the Lord God commanded the man, 'You may freely eat of every tree of the garden; but of the tree of the knowledge of good and evil you shall not eat, for in the day that you eat of it you shall die.' Then the Lord God said, 'It is not good that the man should be alone; I will make him a helper as his partner.' ... So the Lord God caused a deep sleep to fall upon the man, and he slept; then he took one of his ribs and closed up its place with flesh. And the rib that the Lord God had taken from the man he made into a woman and brought her to the man. Then the man said, 'This at last is bone of my bones and flesh of my flesh; this one shall be called Woman, for out of Man this one was taken.' Therefore a man leaves his father and his mother and clings to his wife, and they become one flesh. And the man and his wife were both naked, and were not ashamed.

GENESIS 2:7, 15–18, 21–25

This is the truth sent from above
The truth of God, the God of love
Therefore don't turn me from your door
But hearken all, both rich and poor.

The first thing that I do relate
Is that God did man create
The next thing which to you I'll tell
Woman was made with man to dwell.

And after that, 'twas God's own choice
To place them both in Paradise,
There to remain of evil free
Except they ate of such a tree.

But they did eat, which was a sin,
And so their ruin did begin,
Ruined themselves, both you and me,
And all of their posterity.

Thus we were heirs to endless woes
Till God and Lord did interpose
And so a promise soon did run
That He would redeem us by His Son.

And at that season of the year
Our blessed redeemer did appear
He here did live and here did preach
And many thousands he did teach.

Thus He in love to us behaved
To show us how we must be saved
And if you want to know the way
Be pleased to hear what He did say.

WORDS AND MUSIC: ENGLISH TRADITIONAL

For many people, this carol will always be associated with the opening section of the *Fantasia on Christmas Carols* written by Ralph Vaughan Williams (1872–1958) in 1912. The rather unusual tune was notated by Vaughan Williams, and it has an irregular rhythmic structure, alternating bars of five beats with bars of six. There is no sense of imbalance, however, because it conveys a sense of movement, carrying us forward as the tale unfolds. In this the music complements the long distances in time that the text describes, bringing us from Adam and Eve through to the redeeming work of Jesus. Some versions of the text add verses that take us all the way to Jesus' command to preach the gospel throughout the world (Matthew 28:19).

Vaughan Williams' *Fantasia* is a kind of meditation on Christmas, containing a collection of four carols, emphasizing not only folk music and text but also the popular theology that underlies them. It is a fine seasonal piece, which perhaps suffers from being heard only at Christmas-time.

It begins with a slightly haunting, even mystical introduction on the cello, setting the mood and suggesting that what we are about to hear is not a sentimental medley of well-known Christmas carols. Very soon, the choir enter, singing the carol, 'This is the truth sent from above'. Soloists take verses, while the choir hum underneath in various different ways, and luscious strings interpose phrases between the verses. Thus Vaughan Williams shows us an exquisite example of what he was so good at—musical brushstrokes, illustrating the text.

The *Fantasia* then changes pace, moving into a version of 'Come all you worthy gentlemen', a Herefordshire carol that is reminiscent of 'God rest you merry, gentlemen'. This takes us fully into the story of the birth of Christ, and raises the level of celebration a notch. Rich harmonies and canonical writing (voices entering in succession) lead us forward towards the Sussex Carol ('On Christmas night all Christians sing'). In 6/8 time, it is a dance-like carol, which we hear before the composer reintroduces another verse of 'Come all you worthy gentlemen', and both carols are then sung in tandem, each playing off, bouncing against and even clashing with the other. The effect is never unpleasant, but rather brings a smile as we realize that these two carols have been made to fit together. The final sentiments as the pairing fades away are the wishing of a 'Happy new year'. Thus we might be reminded that this is a carol for the Christmas season, which *begins* on Christmas Day and carries us through New Year, up to Epiphany.

Vaughan Williams composed the *Fantasia on Christmas Carols* during a period in his life when he had been traveling round Britain, avidly collecting folk music, and it was dedicated to Cecil Sharpe (1859–1924), a fellow folksong collector and friend.

The text of the carol 'This is the truth' is all about the history of salvation, taking us right back to the creation of humankind. As in 'Adam lay ybounden', which we shall consider tomorrow, we are reminded that the story of Christ was effectively begun at the moment God created the world. A fallen humanity needs a redeemer, and that was the case from the moment that Adam and Eve sinned, resulting in exile from paradise. Consequently, we, the human race, have been 'heirs to endless woes', even though there arose a promise that one day we would be redeemed. This promise is to be found in the writings of the prophets, especially the later chapters of Isaiah.

From the book of Genesis we see that the creation of human-kind is bound up in the creation of the universe, but also that our behaviour towards and relationships with each other and our environment deeply affect our fate. We have a great deal of freedom and considerable power over our environment, and we have always held this to be so. God grants Adam freedom to eat what he likes, but forbids only one thing, which consequently he and Eve cannot resist. This reminds us that we are still very much responsible for our environment, which is now in a dire situation. Global warming, melting ice caps and carbon dioxide emissions are caused and ignored by humanity to such an extent that some scientists are very seriously worried about what will happen over the next hundred years or so. It has even been suggested that there is a 50 per cent chance that humanity will not survive the 21st century. For Christians, the prospect that a world amenable to human existence might be in its death throes is of great concern, because we know that God created and loved the world that he created, placing humanity upon it. On the other hand, this may mean that the Advent fear and hope of a final tribulation, in the midst of which Christ returns, is not so far-fetched after all.

Prayer

O God of love, who created humanity and placed us in paradise until we were ruined by sin, do not turn us away from your presence, but show us how we must be saved by following in the way of your dear Son Jesus Christ, who was born, lived and died for us, but who now reigns in glory with you and the Holy Spirit, now and for ever. Amen.

ADAM LAY YBOUNDEN

Now the serpent was more crafty than any other wild animal that the Lord God had made. He said to the woman, 'Did God say, "You shall not eat from any tree in the garden"?' The woman said to the serpent, 'We may eat of the fruit of the trees in the garden; but God said, "You shall not eat of the fruit of the tree that is in the middle of the garden, nor shall you touch it, or you shall die."' But the serpent said to the woman, 'You will not die; for God knows that when you eat of it your eyes will be opened, and you will be like God, knowing good and evil.' So when the woman saw that the tree was good for food, and that it was a delight to the eyes, and that the tree was to be desired to make one wise, she took of its fruit and ate; and she also gave some to her husband, who was with her, and he ate. Then the eyes of both were opened, and they knew that they were naked; and they sewed fig leaves together and made loincloths for themselves. They heard the sound of the Lord God walking in the garden at the time of the evening breeze, and the man and his wife hid themselves from the presence of the Lord God among the trees of the garden.

GENESIS 3:1–8

Adam lay ybounden
Bounden in a bond:
Four thousand winter
Thought he not too long.

An all was for an apple,
An apple that he took,
As Clerkes finden
Written in their book.

Ne had the apple taken been,
The apple taken been
Ne had never our Lady
A been heavene queen.

Blessed be the time
That apple taken was;
Therefore we moun singen:
Deo Gracias!

WORDS: 15TH CENTURY
MUSIC: BORIS ORD (1897–1961)

The British Museum is now regarded as one of the greatest of the world. It was founded by an Act of Parliament in 1753, when Sir Hans Sloane bequeathed his collection to King George II. Within that set of original manuscripts was the text of this carol, for which there are many musical settings. The origins of the text cannot be traced much further back than Sloane, but a 15th-century date is widely accepted. The language is clearly post-Chaucerian but pre-Shakespearian. What is of more interest, perhaps, is what the text says and what it does not say. Some of the words need slight translation: '(y)bounden' means 'bound'; 'Clerkes' are clerks, or priests; 'finden' means 'find'; 'ne' means something like 'not if', and 'moun singen' means 'must sing'. '*Deo Gracias*' is Latin for 'Thanks be to God'. The technical term for a carol that uses both Latin and English is 'macaronic'.

For a Christmas carol, we must notice immediately that Jesus is not mentioned at all. Nevertheless, Christ is implicit throughout. The text is about the sin of Adam and Eve, the eating of the forbidden fruit, which the unknown writer takes to be a happy precursor of the salvation wrought for humankind in and through Christ. The logic is unequivocal: if Adam had not disobeyed God, then humanity would not have fallen into sin; and if that had not happened, we would not have needed redemption. And if we had not needed redemption, there would have been no need for God to send Christ to redeem us, and that means that not only would there have been no crucifixion and resurrection, there would have been no incarnation—no nativity, no Christmas! The implication is that we would be worse off for having nothing to thank God for. It is almost as if the sin of Adam were a good thing, because it enabled God to do wondrous deeds in Christ; to make Mary the queen of heaven (a Catholic doctrine of the period, still held by some Roman Catholics today), and to give us something to sing about.

The reverse logic that we find in this carol does raise some theological conundrums. The apostle Paul famously wrote, 'For since death came through a human being, the resurrection of the dead has also come through a human being; for as all die in Adam, so all will be made alive in Christ. But each in his own order: Christ the first fruits, then at his coming those who belong to Christ' (1 Corinthians 15:21–23).

The idea here is that because Adam sinned, humanity was fallen; and Christ, the 'second Adam', reverses the damage done by that sin by redeeming humanity. The theologian and poet John Henry Newman (1801–90) summed this up beautifully in what became the hymn 'Praise to the holiest':

> O loving wisdom of our God!
> When all was sin and shame,
> A second Adam to the fight
> And to the rescue came.

The writer of 'Adam lay ybounden' has turned this idea around, thereby falling into the philosophical trap of presuming that a statement containing a counterfactual can have a truth-value! This means that a statement containing the word 'if' cannot be treated for logical purposes as though it were true. I might say, for example, 'If it had not rained I would not have got wet', but because the truth of such a statement cannot be verified (it *did* rain, so how can we know what would have happened if it had not done so?), the statement must be deemed to be false. Thus, while it appears to make sense to say that if it had not rained I would not have got wet, we should not treat this as a logically true statement, because it cannot be verified. It is extremely *likely* that I would not have got wet, but it cannot be *true*. It is conceivable that I might have got wet by some other means (someone might have thrown a bucket of water at me).

Such technicalities of language and logic do help us to conclude that the idea that if Adam had not sinned, Jesus would not have come is actually absurd. It is certainly unverifiable and, strictly speaking, is false. Who knows what God would have done? And who are we to decide or guess?

Having demolished the writer's logic, we should at least give credit where it is due: the text is at root a hymn of praise and gratitude to God. The words celebrate the history of salvation and end on a note of thanksgiving. The Bible passage from which the carol draws its inspiration reminds us of the 'original' sin of Adam and Eve, whose story shows how easy it is to be tempted by something, especially if it is marketed well. The serpent also uses a certain form of bogus philosophy, based on the idea that if something is forbidden, that must be because it is interesting, and will not do harm but good. Adam and Eve have the maker's instructions to hand, but they prefer the do-it-yourself approach of the snake. Of course, they botch it up, not only for themselves but for all who follow them. And that is why God has to send Christ as redeemer, cleanser and restorer, for which we continue to give him thanks and praise: 'For just as by the one man's disobedience the many were made sinners, so by the one man's obedience the many will be made righteous' (Romans 5:19).

Boris Ord, who wrote the most famous setting of 'Adam lay

ybounden', was Director of Music at King's College, Cambridge, between 1929 and 1957. This is his only published piece of music, and it was written for the 'Festival of Nine Lessons and Carols', which was adapted in 1918 by Eric Milner White, then Dean of King's College, Cambridge, from a service originally created in 1880 by E.H. Benson. The service was first used in a wooden shed that served as a church in Cornwall. Benson became Archbishop of Canterbury, and the building became Truro Cathedral. This order of service, which has found its way to all corners of the world, traces the story of salvation, musically and scripturally, beginning with Adam's sin and culminating in the account of the incarnation found in John's Gospel. 'Adam lay ybounden' was therefore an obvious text for Ord to pick, and his setting is relatively simple to sing, and is much-loved and sung today.

There are other settings of this carol that are worth mentioning briefly, one written in 1956 by John Ireland and another by Peter Warlock (real name Philip Heseltine), both of which survive into contemporary use. Another version appears in that fine collection known as the 'Ceremony of Carols', which Benjamin Britten wrote in 1942. The eight carols with processional and recessional 'Hodie Christus Natus Est' ('Today Jesus Christ is born') are for treble voices alone, accompanied by a harp. In that work, the title of the carol is 'Deo Gracias' ('Thanks be to God'), and it begins with an exclamation of those words of gratitude. While we may question the rest of the text for the assumptions that it makes, we can hardly argue with the thanksgiving with which it concludes: thanks be to God!

Prayer

Father God, we thank you that you sent your Son Jesus to rescue us from the shame of sin and the fear of death. By your gracious Spirit, teach us the truth of the story of salvation, that we may be released from the bonds of fallen humanity, always free to offer you thanks and praise, this and every day. Amen.

O COME, O COME, EMMANUEL!

Take heed, be quiet, do not fear, and do not let your heart be faint because of these two smouldering stumps of firebrands, because of the fierce anger of Rezin and Aram and the son of Remaliah... On that day the root of Jesse shall stand as a signal to the peoples; the nations shall inquire of him, and his dwelling shall be glorious... I will place on his shoulder the key of the house of David; he shall open, and no one shall shut; he shall shut, and no one shall open...

But for you who revere my name the sun of righteousness shall rise, with healing in its wings. You shall go out leaping like calves from the stall.

ISAIAH 7:4; 11:10; 22:22; MALACHI 4:2

O come, O come, Emmanuel!
Redeem thy captive Israel,
That into exile drear is gone
Far from the face of God's dear Son.
Rejoice! Rejoice! Emmanuel
Shall come to thee, O Israel.

O come, thou Wisdom from on high!
Who madest all in earth and sky,
Creating man from dust and clay:
To us reveal salvation's way.

O come, O come, Adonai,
Who in thy glorious majesty
From Sinai's mountain, clothed with awe,
Gavest thy folk the ancient law.

O come, thou Root of Jesse! draw
The quarry from the lion's claw;
From those dread caverns of the grave,
From nether hell, thy people save.

O come, thou Lord of David's Key!
The royal door fling wide and free;
Safeguard for us the heavenward road,
And bar the way to death's abode.

O come, O come, thou Dayspring bright!
Pour on our souls thy healing light;
Dispel the long night's lingering gloom,
And pierce the shadows of the tomb.

O come, Desire of nations! show
Thy kingly reign on earth below;
Thou Cornerstone, uniting all,
Restore the ruin of our fall.

WORDS: 18TH CENTURY, TRANS. T.A. LACEY (1853–1931)
MUSIC: *VENI EMMANUEL*, ADAPTED FROM A FRENCH MISSAL BY THOMAS HELMORE (1811–90)

This season of Advent not only has us looking forward to the return of Christ, but we also look back in order to look forward. The birth of Jesus was itself looked forward to, and as we remind ourselves that he is due to return, we remember some of those prophecies that were to predict his birth in Bethlehem. Not only do they come from the Old Testament, but some of them became enshrined as antiphons (brief texts for liturgical use before and after canticles) even after the New Testament period. The Magnificat is said or sung every day at Evening Prayer, but in the run-up to Christmas, these special verses (the 'Advent antiphons'), recalling the prophecies associated with Mary's acceptance of her calling to be the mother of Jesus, were added, giving extra poignancy to the oft-sung text. There is therefore a slight irony in the fact that while 'O come, O come, Emmanuel' is a great Advent hymn, it is not ideally suited to the beginning of Advent after all. It is most appropriate as an end-of-Advent hymn, to be sung when one of the verses might coincide with the appropriate antiphon for the particular day.

The antiphons date from the sixth or seventh century, and there were seven of them, according to this scheme:

17 December: *O Sapientia*

O Wisdom, which camest out of the mouth of the Most High, and reachest from one end to another, mightily and sweetly ordering all things: come and teach us the way of prudence.

18 December: *O Adonai*

O Adonai, and Leader of the house of Israel, who appearedst in the bush to Moses in a flame of fire, and gavest him the Law in Sinai: come and deliver us with an outstretched arm.

19 December: *O Radix Jesse*

O Root of Jesse, which standest for an ensign of the people, at whom kings shall shut their mouths, to whom the Gentiles shall seek: come and deliver us, and tarry not.

20 December: *O Clavis David*

O Key of David and Sceptre of the house of Israel; that openest, and no man shutteth, and shuttest, and no man openeth: come and bring the prisoner out of the prisonhouse, and him that sitteth in darkness and the shadow of death.

21 December: *O Oriens*

O Dayspring, Brightness of Light Everlasting, and Sun of Righteousness: come and enlighten him that sitteth in darkness and the shadow of death.

22 December: *O Rex Gentium*

O King of the Nations, and their Desire; the Cornerstone, who makest both one: come and save mankind, whom thou formedst of clay.

23 December: *O Emmanuel*

O Emmanuel, our King and Lawgiver, the Desire of all nations, and their Salvation: come and save us, O Lord our God.

The texts of the antiphons themselves are rich in meaning and resonate with scripture. Each addresses God by a different name. Wisdom, the first name to be used, draws on a great tradition in the Bible of personifying the figure of Wisdom in feminine terms: 'Happy are those who find wisdom, and those who get under-standing, for her income is better than silver, and her revenue better than gold' (Proverbs 3:13–14; see also 4:6–9). The desire for the character of Wisdom to teach us is very much in the tradition of the book of Proverbs.

The antiphon *O Adonai* refers to the Hebrew name for God (Lord), and reminds us of the encounter of Moses with God in the burning bush (Exodus 3) and of the giving of the tablets of the Ten Commandments (see Deuteronomy 9:9–10). The outstretched arm reminds us of God telling Moses to stretch out his arm each time a plague was to befall the Egyptians, and ultimately of God showing strength with his arm in releasing them (see Exodus 7:5). The same idea of God's powerful arm is mentioned by Mary in the Magnificat (Luke 1:51).

The root of Jesse is mentioned in Isaiah 11:10 and the key of David in Isaiah 22:22. The 'shadow of death' reminds us of Psalm 23 and the release of the prisoners reminds us of Jesus quoting Isaiah 61 in Luke 4:18. 'Dayspring' is a word often associated with dawn, as in Zechariah's prophecy uttered at the birth of John the Baptist (Luke 1:78), and also with the idea of Christ as the 'morning star'. Christ as cornerstone is a familiar phrase, found in Ephesians 2:20 and 1 Peter 2:6. The final 'O Emmanuel' antiphon is the climactic one, resounding as it does with the prophecy from Isaiah 7:14: 'The young woman... shall name him Immanuel'.

These Latin 'Advent antiphons', as they became known, evolved into the hymn 'Veni, veni, Emmanuel', of which various translations of 'O come, O come, Emmanuel' are the surviving English versions. The first translation was made by Cardinal John Henry Newman in 1836, and John Mason Neale followed suit in 1851. It is actually his own revision of these words that we find in some hymn books, while the words printed here are taken from a different text used in the New English Hymnal. Mason's version had five verses only, whereas this version quoted has the full complement of seven. Just as Latin antiphons served as a kind of refrain to the Magnificat when the hymn was created, around the twelfth century, the hymn itself was given a refrain: 'Gaude, gaude Emmanuel, nascitur pro te, Israel' ('Rejoice, rejoice...'). In a sense, then, this hymn is a set of refrains, with a refrain!

It is quite unusual these days to sing all of these verses, and, as already noted, many hymn books do not even contain them all. If all the verses are sung, it can become quite a marathon of music, taking many minutes and taxing the voice of anyone who sings 'Rejoice' with any gusto! The 'O' antiphons (or 'Great Os'), as they are sometimes called (because they all begin with 'O...'), can be sung in procession or with interludes of readings, thus turning the hymn into a celebration of the various hopes invested in the Messiah. Breaking the hymn up in this way can not only make it easier to sing, but also helps to create a sense of dramatic narrative as music and text interlace. Combined with a candlelit procession, this can be a very powerful part of any Advent liturgy.

The tune itself is derived from a French medieval plainsong melody, which was possibly used as a tune for *Kyrie Eleison* ('Lord, have mercy'), the opening part of a sung eucharist. While there have been differences of opinion over the texts of the hymn, there has been no argument over the use of its distinctive tune. The most commonly used version of the tune was arranged by Thomas Helmore, an Anglican clergyman who helped revive interest in plainsong (Gregorian chant) in the 19th century. Often today we hear the hymn with verses sung in unison, rather as the plainsong would have been, but with rich harmony used for the refrains. This may represent for us something of the complex blend that makes up today's Advent. There is the simple, penitential message of a promised saviour, who came and will come again, but there is also the richness and splendour of Christmas, beckoning us from every shop window and carol service as we advance further into December.

Prayer

O come Emmanuel, Key of David, Root of Jesse, Dayspring on high, and reveal yourself as Lord of all the nations. To you we call, Lord Jesus, whose name is above all names, rejoicing in the salvation that you have won for us by your humble birth, sacrificial death and glorious resurrection. May you reign in glory, in heaven and on earth, now and always. Amen.

VENI, VENI, EMMANUEL

'When you see Jerusalem surrounded by armies, then know that its desolation has come near. Then those in Judea must flee to the mountains, and those inside the city must leave it, and those out in the country must not enter it; for these are days of vengeance, as a fulfilment of all that is written. Woe to those who are pregnant and to those who are nursing infants in those days! For there will be great distress on the earth and wrath against this people; they will fall by the edge of the sword and be taken away as captives among all nations; and Jerusalem will be trampled on by the Gentiles, until the times of the Gentiles are fulfilled.

'There will be signs in the sun, the moon, and the stars, and on the earth distress among nations confused by the roaring of the sea and the waves. People will faint from fear and foreboding of what is coming upon the world, for the powers of the heavens will be shaken. Then they will see "the Son of Man coming in a cloud" with power and great glory. Now when these things begin to take place, stand up and raise your heads, because your redemption is drawing near.'

LUKE 21:20–28

'O come, O come, Emmanuel' has inspired a great deal of music. It is the hymn that we most associate with Advent, so much so that we only have to hear a few notes from it to be reminded of the season. I remember the first time I preached in St Paul's Cathedral after having gone there in 1998 as Succentor. My lot fell to preach at a Sunday eucharist in the middle of August, and the text for the service was a well-known Advent text, Luke 12:32–40 (See 'Thou whose almighty Word', p. 49). As is the usual custom in large cathedrals, the gospel book is carried down the nave, so that it is read from within the body of the congregation after Alleluias have been sung. This done, the small procession makes its way back to the altar, and the preacher climbs the steps to the pulpit, which is raised about ten feet off the ground. While these very practical liturgical movements are taking place, it is traditional for the organist to improvise, playing music that forms his or her personal response to what has been read.

On this August day in question, John Scott, organist at the time, was playing, and as the procession returned to the altar and I made my hesitant way up the steps for the first time, he played gently, but recognizably, the first few notes of the tune of 'O come, O come, Emmanuel'. The congregation would have been taken by surprise, undoubtedly, it being summertime, but then the music moved away from the theme and built up, until after about two minutes the theme returned, with other notes flying all around, a trumpet blazing 'O come, O come, Emmanuel' through sparkling notes of summer. By this time, I was in the pulpit, admiring the virtuosity, the inventiveness and the profundity of this musical commentary on what had just been read. As I stood there, looking down the length of St Paul's, I wondered if there really was any point in saying anything, for in a way it had already all been said with the voice of the organ. While there is no recording of that brief moment of musical theology, it is one of my abiding memories of ministering in that unique and special place. Such can be the power of meaningful music.

A very similar and more prolonged effect has been achieved by the Scottish composer James MacMillan (b. 1959). His concerto *Veni, Veni, Emmanuel*, composed for the percussionist Evelyn Glennie and given its first performance at the Proms in 1992, is also a musical-theological reflection on the Advent season. Evelyn Glennie is reckoned to be the world's first solo percussionist, who began her musical career at the age of eight when she took the Associated Board Grade One piano exam, achieving the highest mark ever awarded. What is notable about her is that she is deaf, and has to practise and perform by feeling musical vibrations through the air and floor.

MacMillan's *Veni, Veni, Emmanuel* is a remarkable piece, and in the first eight years of its life was performed over 200 times in 27 countries. It is a percussion concerto, and the success and speed with which it has been taken up by orchestras and audiences must make it one of the most popular 20th-century concertos. The first recording with Evelyn Glennie is still very much admired (CD order code: BMG 09026–61916), but a live performance is also a visual event, as the soloist has to do quite a lot of running around among banks of drums, bells and mallet instruments. What is most striking about it, however, given its success, is the spiritual depth of the piece.

MacMillan began writing it on Advent Sunday 1991 and it was completed on Easter Day 1992. These dates give a clue to the work's meaning, for while it is a musical attempt to reflect theologically on the meaning of Advent, Macmillan's vision also carries us through to Easter resurrection. His music (there is no text or singing) deals with some of the themes of Advent, but brings us at the end to a glittering, bell-ringing Easter climax. The final minutes of the work evoke the kind of bell-ringing that precedes the singing of the *Gloria* on Easter Eve, as choir and congregation welcome the risen Christ.

But there is much preceding this happy ending to MacMillan's apocalypse. The passage from Luke 21 is the key to the work, reminding us of the calamity that will precede the second coming, and while there is much beauty in MacMillan's work, there are times when the banging and crashing of percussion might remind us of the clamour of the end-time. All of the musical material is based on the plainchant '*Veni, Veni, Emmanuel*', but there is also a strong spiritual meaning coursing through the music, pushed by a 'heartbeat', which MacMillan says represents the human presence of Christ. The final, coda, section, which is subtitled 'Easter', reminds us that it is the risen Christ of whom we are speaking. We should never forget that the Christ of the second coming is, of course, the *risen* Christ, and it is in the risen Christ that we find the realization of the 'liberation' referred to by Luke.

We begin with Advent, though, with percussionist and orchestra in dialogue, playing with rhythms and sound-effects, fanfares reminiscent perhaps of the last trumpet, and an ensuing chaos. Soon some order asserts itself and we realize that we are to be led on a conversation-journey in which we often hear snatches of the familiar plainsong, sometimes tantalizingly brief, at other times distracted by percussive brilliance. As the central section of the work approaches, a tranquillity sets in, and then we begin to recognize the notes of the refrain from the hymn '*Gaude*' (Rejoice!). Thus the theme itself becomes almost a symbol of the Advent season. Just as we may feel we can glimpse the return of Christ, or have some sense of its reality, sometimes it is barely detectable or believable, and this sense can be felt in the music. The theme tune never completely disappears, and occasionally, especially towards the end, it can be heard in blatant form. There is also a sense throughout the work that while we may strain to identify the theme, we know it will return to satisfy our musical need for completeness. It is often the case that a piece of music sets up tensions that only it can resolve, and this is why we often find music so satisfying. There are things we need to hear, resolutions that we need to experience, all defined by the internal logic of harmony and melody.

In this we have a metaphor for the nativity and return of Christ. God sent his Son Jesus Christ as the harmonic resolution of the discord and cacophony of human sin. Yet the glories of incarnation produced only a partial resolution, interrupted and tainted by crucifixion and redeemed through resurrection. This closure on the eighth day of creation, when Christ rose and made all things new, breaking the chains of death and setting his people free, has yet to be fully realized. There are notes still to be played, chords yet to sound in the great concerto that is the dialogue between God and Creation. In this 'middle' time, between Easter salvation and final return, we have plenty of music resounding in our ears, but we need some melodic and harmonic resolutions to make all things good, and to complete the whole.

This is what Advent is about, and it is what impels us to sing, at any time of year, 'O come, O come, Emmanuel'!

Prayer

Shake the powers of heaven, O Lord, with drumbeats of glory, and rain down upon us the glittering light of your love, so that the beats of our hearts may reverberate in anticipation of the eternal dialogue you have prepared for us, when heaven and earth shall pass away and all shall enter into the everlasting harmony of your kingdom. Amen.

ONCE IN ROYAL DAVID'S CITY

In those days a decree went out from Emperor Augustus that all the world should be registered. This was the first registration and was taken while Quirinius was governor of Syria. All went to their own towns to be registered. Joseph also went from the town of Nazareth in Galilee to Judea, to the city of David called Bethlehem, because he was descended from the house and family of David. He went to be registered with Mary, to whom he was engaged and who was expecting a child. While they were there, the time came for her to deliver her child. And she gave birth to her firstborn son and wrapped him in bands of cloth, and laid him in a manger, because there was no place for them in the inn.

LUKE 2:1–7

Once in royal David's city
Stood a lowly cattle shed,
Where a mother laid her baby
In a manger for his bed;
Mary was the mother mild,
Jesus Christ her little child.

He came down to earth from heaven
Who is God and Lord of all;
And his shelter was a stable,
And his cradle was a stall;
With the poor and mean and lowly
Lived on earth our Saviour holy.

And through all his wondrous childhood
He would honour and obey,
Love and watch the lowly maiden,
In whose gentle arms he lay:
Christian children all must be
Mild, obedient, good as he.

For he is our childhood's pattern,
Day by day like us he grew;
He was little, weak and helpless,
Tears and smiles like us he knew;
And he feeleth for our sadness,
And he shareth in our gladness.

And our eyes at last shall see him,
Through his own redeeming love;
For that child so dear and gentle
Is our Lord in heaven above;
And he leads his children on
To the place where he is gone.

Not in that poor lowly stable,
With the oxen standing by
We shall see him; but in heaven,
Set at God's right hand on high
Where like stars, his children crowned
All in white shall wait around.

WORDS: C.F. ALEXANDER (1818–95)
MUSIC: IRBY, H.J. GAUNTLETT (1805–76)

My mother tells me that my entry into the world on this day in 1966
was hastened by an attempt to move a twin-tub washing machine.
Such strenuous efforts late in pregnancy can bring about labour and,
in my case, premature birth. Apparently the umbilical cord had got

tangled round my neck and it was a close-run thing that I survived at all. If I had not been born early, I might not have been born at all, so to speak.

Birth itself is a miracle, enfleshed millions of times each year in so many places and ways. Clinics with water-birth pools and the latest technologies are *de rigeur* all over the Western world, and mothers are given lessons in pain management, advised to have 'birthing partners' and are generally informed (sometimes too much) about what is going on and what could go wrong. The jargon of 'epidural', 'c-section' and 'TENS machine' is so familiar to expectant mums these days and, as with many things, the intention is to facilitate choice and control. Pregnancy and childbirth are far safer than they used to be, but there is still a fair bit of trepidation about!

In some less technologically equipped parts of the world, giving birth is little different from the way it would have been in first-century Palestine. There is no maternity leave or benefit (no 'job' to have leave from!), and only certain cultures promote rest for the expectant mum. Back in first-century Palestine, poor Mary had to trek from Nazareth to Bethlehem, a journey of about 70 miles (100km). After bouncing along on a beast of burden for up to ten days, it is little surprise that her labour began and she was soon delivered of her Saviour son (but note that there is no mention of a donkey in the Gospel narratives). It makes one wonder whether Jesus was born prematurely.

It was not so different in the middle of the 19th century, when Frances Alexander was writing 'Once in royal David's city'. Victorian England had a high rate of infant mortality: in Sheffield, for example, the General Infirmary recorded 11,944 deaths between 1837 and 1842, half of which were of children under the age of five. Statistics such as these help us to understand part of the spiritual agenda of this carol. With so many children dying young, the verses at the end of the carol can be seen in a different light. To us today, the idea that Jesus 'leads his children' to heaven, where 'all in white' they wait around, crowned as angels, is a rather strange, sentimental, even unsatisfactory picture of heaven. But to those many who had lost little ones, these words provided some comfort, convincing them that those brief lives were not in vain.

Some people today feel that the words are too outdated for modern use. The idea that 'Christian children all must be mild, obedient, good as he' rankles with some worshippers, as such sentiments are redolent of the Victorian Sunday school with its dry biblical teaching through catechism and discipline (although one might ask why children should *not* be obedient). Mrs Alexander was trying to help, not only by writing singable hymns but also by conveying essential Christian truths through her words. 'Once in royal David's city' was specifically intended to teach that major part of the creed: 'I believe in Jesus Christ, his only Son our Lord, who was conceived by the Holy Spirit, born of the Virgin Mary'. In writing this carol, she demonstrated both her love of children and her understanding of the humanity of Christ. Like many youth workers today, her heart was very much in the mission and evangelization of young people, always striving to bring the gospel up to date for each and every generation.

Her words, whether we consider them old-fashioned or not, are rich in scriptural overtones. While the first verse sets out in straightforward terms the circumstances of Christ's birth, the second stanza introduces a reference to the kenotic (self-emptying) Christ that we encounter in Philippians 2:5–8 (see 'In the bleak mid-winter', 30 December, p. 161). The stanza goes on to remind us of Christ's earthly poverty, as referred to in 2 Corinthians 8:9: 'though he was rich, yet for your sakes he became poor, so that by his poverty you might become rich'. The next verse reminds us of Jesus' sinlessness, as set out in 1 John 3:5: 'You know that he was revealed to take away sins, and in him there is no sin'. Though sinless, he was also human: thus, like us, he knew of the joys and pains (tears and smiles) of human existence, and this is touched upon in the fourth verse.

The fifth verse reminds us of the end of the story, of Christ risen, ascended, glorified (Luke 24:50–53; Acts 1:6–14). Christ reigning in heaven is not a childish fantasy but a scriptural truth. 'All in white, who wait around' is perhaps an unfortunate description of those who have had their robes washed in the blood of the lamb (Revelation 4:4; 7:14), but it is clearly Mrs Alexander's pastoral vision that the souls of deceased children go to be with God, casting their star-like crowns before him as they enjoy the eternal bliss of heaven. It may be a mawkish vision with which to conclude a delightful and enduring hymn, but it is perhaps churlish to omit this verse, as it points us, firmly rooted in the earthbound stable, upwards to that higher, purer place where there shall be no more tears—a new heaven and earth, presided over by our Lord Jesus Christ (Revelation 21:1–4).

Frances Alexander (known as 'Fanny') actually wrote most of her hymns before she was married in 1850, publishing a volume in 1848 called *Hymns for Little Children*. She gave away to charity almost all of the money she earned from writing, helping to establish an institute for the deaf in Strabane, Northern Ireland. Her husband, William Alexander, was an Irish Anglican who, after Fanny's death, became Archbishop of Armagh in Northern Ireland. On the day of her funeral, in October 1885, the shops were closed, 92 clergymen attended, and the streets of Londonderry (as it is now known) were full of mourners. Other hymns that she wrote which are still very much in use include 'All things bright and beautiful' and 'There is a green hill far away'.

The well-loved tune IRBY was composed by Henry Gauntlett for these words soon after they were written, and so the carol first appeared with the tune in 1849, and made it into the first edition of *Hymns Ancient and Modern* in 1861.

Prayer

Father God, whose Son Jesus Christ came down to earth from heaven, hear our prayers for all who are weak and helpless. By the power of your redeeming love, lead us your children to share in the gladness of that day when all tears shall be turned to smiles in your heavenly city, where, with saints and angels attending, you reign in glory for ever. Amen.

GABRIEL'S MESSAGE

In the sixth month the angel Gabriel was sent by God to a town in Galilee called Nazareth, to a virgin engaged to a man whose name was Joseph, of the house of David. The virgin's name was Mary. And he came to her and said, 'Greetings, favoured one! The Lord is with you.' But she was much perplexed by his words and pondered what sort of greeting this might be. The angel said to her, 'Do not be afraid, Mary, for you have found favour with God. And now, you will conceive in your womb and bear a son, and you will name him Jesus. He will be great, and will be called the Son of the Most High, and the Lord God will give to him the throne of his ancestor David. He will reign over the house of Jacob for ever, and of his kingdom there will be no end.' Mary said to the angel, 'How can this be, since I am a virgin?' The angel said to her, 'The Holy Spirit will come upon you, and the power of the Most High will overshadow you; therefore the child to be born will be holy; he will be called Son of God. And now, your relative Elizabeth in her old age has also conceived a son; and this is the sixth month for her who was said to be barren. For nothing will be impossible with God.' Then Mary said, 'Here am I, the servant of the Lord; let it be with me according to your word.' Then the angel departed from her.

LUKE 1:26–38

The angel Gabriel from heaven came,
his wings as drifted snow, his eyes as flame
'All hail,' said he, 'thou lowly maiden Mary,
most highly favoured lady!' Gloria!

'For lo! a blessed Mother thou shalt be,
all generations laud and honour thee.
Thy Son shall be Emmanuel, by seers foretold,
most highly favoured lady!' Gloria!

Then gentle Mary meekly bowed her head;
'To me be as it pleaseth God,' she said;
'My soul shall laud and magnify his holy name.'
Most highly favoured lady! Gloria!

Of her, Emmanuel, the Christ, was born
in Bethlehem, all on a Christmas morn.
And Christian folk throughout the world will ever say,
'Most highly favoured lady!' Gloria!

WORDS: SABINE BARING GOULD (1834–1924)
MUSIC: BASQUE TRADITIONAL

Waiting for a baby to be born is a strange experience, though in different ways for mother and father. For both parents there is a kind of unreality: it seems it can't be really happening, even though, as every day goes by, the physical evidence becomes more real. It is strange enough for us today, knowing how babies develop in the womb, and able to take advantage of hospitals, midwives and scanning machines, all of which can confirm or dispel hopes or fears, but what must it have been like for Mary and Joseph? Everything about her pregnancy was unusual and surreal. When Gabriel told Mary she was pregnant, did she have any sense that it might be true? Did Gabriel's message somehow confirm the queasiness she had been feeling of late? Or did it somehow not relate to what her own body was telling her? If it didn't, it soon would!

For Mary, like any human mother, the idea and manifestation of pregnancy is natural, but utterly strange. Her body would be taken over by another being, growing, moving, becoming, inside her. As time went by, the spiritual words of an angel would be confirmed by the physical kicking of a human baby. Church tradition dates the Feast of the Annunciation to March 25, a very precise nine months before December 25! And in Luke's Gospel we read that the angel tells Mary that her cousin Elizabeth is now in her 'sixth month'. If this is all correct, then Jesus would have been born nine months later, and John the Baptist would then have been six months old.

Mary's response to the angel, which has been handed on to us as the Magnificat ('My soul magnifies the Lord...'), is an inspiring profession of faith and acceptance. Mary's 'yes' to God has helped generations to be strong, committed and resolute in the face of poverty, war, persecution and doubt. As her body accepts the inevitable restrictions and discomforts that childbearing will involve, her spirit also affirms the route on which she and the whole of humanity are about to embark. The journey she makes through pregnancy involves her children's children, spiritually speaking. In bearing the child of God, she reminds us that we are the children of God, spiritually descended from the same heavenly Father.

There are quotations from the Magnificat to be found in this carol, in the third verse. In a brief, two-minute piece of music, we have the heart of the annunciation story. We hear of Gabriel arriving and telling Mary the good news, and there is a lovely foretaste of the later visitation to the shepherds as the refrain *Gloria* is used at the end of each verse. The annunciation is the first step towards that day when the angels will sing 'glory', and all humanity join in, as the promised Messiah, the Emmanuel, the Saviour, is born. While the carol is rooted in the scriptural text, there is an opening out in the last verse, where the focus moves away from describing the event of the annunciation to the angel telling Mary that one day 'Christian folk throughout the world will ever say, "Most highly favoured lady!"' This brings the story into the present, just as we have been taken to the past in remembering that very strange and disconcerting message that Gabriel brought her, all those years ago.

The words come from a traditional Basque carol, and were translated by the Reverend Sabine Baring Gould, author of the hymn 'Onward, Christian soldiers'. He had spent a winter in the

Basque territory, which straddles France and Spain, as a young boy. The gentle, biblical spirituality of these words reveals another side of his character. After ordination, in 1872, he became rector of Lew Trenchard in Devon, where he and his Yorkshire-born wife settled. They had 14 children, but he also found time to study the folksongs of the south-west of England, and to write novels and a 16-volume *Lives of the Saints*.

The charming tune of 'Gabriel's message' also originates in the Basque region. There are various versions and harmonizations of it, the most common being the one by Sir David Willcocks. The rhythmic structure of the carol is unusual, as we hear first a bar in 9/8 time and then one in 12/8 time. This means that there are three beats in the first bar and four in the second. Each of the beats is divisible into three (hence nine and twelve). The effect of this is to convey a stable movement, giving both direction and a certain rootedness, but there is also a sense of slowing up at the end of each of the first two lines. Thereafter the rhythm is constant until the end of the verse. This all adds up to create a lilting effect, which always moves us on, giving a sense of urgency, but because the music is built to withstand this kind of movement, there is never a sense of rushing.

As with the story of salvation itself, there is both control and a certain inevitability and pace to the proceedings. This is heady stuff, we might feel, enough to make anyone jumpy, but all is kept on the rails by a sure, steady foundation of faith, on which Mary herself is drawn along. Her example gives us the confidence to believe and the desire to follow.

Prayer

Heavenly Father, as you sent an angel to Mary bearing good news for all people, enlighten and enrich us with the good news of your love for us all; and as we are reminded of the birth of your Son Jesus Christ, come and dwell in our hearts, that we too may leap to your voice and live our lives in the steady rhythm of mercy on which our faith is founded. Amen.

AVE MARIA

In those days Mary set out and went with haste to a Judean town in the hill country, where she entered the house of Zechariah and greeted Elizabeth. When Elizabeth heard Mary's greeting, the child leapt in her womb. And Elizabeth was filled with the Holy Spirit and exclaimed with a loud cry, 'Blessed are you among women, and blessed is the fruit of your womb. And why has this happened to me, that the mother of my Lord comes to me? For as soon as I heard the sound of your greeting, the child in my womb leapt for joy. And blessed is she who believed that there would be a fulfilment of what was spoken to her by the Lord.'
LUKE 1:39–45

Ave Maria, gratia plena, Dominus tecum, benedicta tu in mulieribus, et benedictus fructus ventris tui, Jesus. (Sancta Maria, Mater Dei, ora pro nobis peccatoribus, nunc et in hora mortis nostrae. Amen.)

Hail Mary, full of grace, the Lord is with thee. Blessed art thou amongst women and blessed is the fruit of thy womb Jesus. (Holy Mary, Mother of God, pray for us sinners, now and at the hour of our death. Amen.)

This text must be one of the most used in Western music, not only because of its central place in Roman Catholic devotion but also because of its pastoral, maternal and thoroughly human focus. Whatever we may think of the theological controversies that surround its meaning and direction, there is no doubt that the *Ave Maria* has inspired and comforted countless generations of Christians.

In order to make up our own minds about what we think of it, we need to divide it into three parts. Firstly, the opening words come from Luke 1:28: 'Greetings, favoured one! The Lord is with you.' These are the words with which the angel Gabriel greets Mary at the annunciation (see 'Gabriel's message', 20 December, p. 110). The second part quotes Elizabeth's words: 'Blessed are you among women, and blessed is the fruit of your womb' (v. 42). To this has been added the name of Jesus. The third section is the most controversial, as it has little if any scriptural origin. The Roman Catholic Council of Trent determined in the 16th century that the phrase 'Holy Mary, Mother of God, pray for us now and at the hour of our death' was composed by the church, while the term 'Mother of God' originated in the Council of Ephesus in AD431 and was used in the Creed of Chalcedon. The purpose then was not so much to elevate the status of Mary as 'God bearer' (theotokos), but to emphasize the truly dual nature of Christ as divine and human.

Many people feel uneasy with the Hail Mary, as praying 'to' the Virgin Mary is implied in the prayer. Christ is our intercessor, and it is he through whom our prayers are offered: 'Consequently he is able for all time to save those who approach God through him, since he always lives to make intercession for them' (Hebrews 7:25). In Protestant and Reformed Christian theology, there is simply no need to offer prayers either to or through the Virgin Mary, and so, while some people find no need for the Hail Mary in their devotions, others are offended by it.

The theological hang-up that Jesus' mother sometimes inspires can so easily lead us away from some very simple truths about the young girl from Nazareth whom God called to be the mother of his Son, Jesus Christ our Saviour. She accepts God's call and we have every reason to believe that her ensuing pregnancy is a normal one, lasting nine months, during which she pays a visit to her cousin Elizabeth. All that is recorded are the words of Elizabeth, praising Mary and expressing delight at her visit. We might also imagine them having the kind of conversation that any two pregnant women might have—a frank and friendly exchange of anecdotes, hopes and fears. The details of such a conversation are not available to us, but the complete humanity of both women encourages us to assume that their encounter was one of mutual support, admiration and humility. We do know a little of their conversation, though, as recorded by Luke. Elizabeth is clearly delighted and honoured that Mary has paid her a visit, not only because they are related but because she recognizes in Mary someone who has received a very special blessing from God. This is therefore a double encounter: two cousins meet, but also two women of faith are blessed in meeting each other.

There is a third dimension too, for it could be said that this is the first time that Jesus and John the Baptist are in the same place at the same time. While we notice their mothers relishing their meeting, we might look forward to the roles that their sons will fulfil, as forerunner and saviour. While Elizabeth tells Mary that the child within her is blessed, a very similar thing can be said of John, whom she carries. These two women are the mothers-to-be of two great men: John, of whom Jesus says, 'among those born of women no one has arisen greater' (Matthew 11:11); and Jesus, of whom John says, 'I am not worthy to untie the thong of his sandal' (John 1:27). The grace and humility with which Jesus and John are later to speak of each other appears to have been inherited from their mothers, whose gracious encounter sets the spiritual tone for the relationship that is yet to begin.

It therefore comes as no surprise that the *Ave Maria* has inspired some beautiful music. Many composers have used it, and the versions by Schubert and Gounod are probably the best-known today. Choral versions exist too, such as the sublime setting by the 16th-century composer Robert Parsons, which opens with a haunting tenor solo and concludes with an extended Amen. Written for six-part choir, it employs only the first two (biblical) parts of the text, thereby avoiding any controversy over the origins of the third section. The brief but equally beautiful setting attributed to the 16th-century Spanish composer Tomás Luis de Victoria includes the full text. Other settings of the *Ave Maria* include that of Anton

Bruckner (1824–96), a devout Austrian Catholic, whose un-accompanied choral setting includes the full text, but has an early climax on the name of Jesus, reminding us that however respectful of Mary we might want to be, Jesus Christ is the focus of our faith.

An unlikely composer of an *Ave Maria* is Igor Stravinsky (1882–1971), as he never professed any particular allegiance to faith. The Russian Orthodox musical tradition informs his setting, which is less than two minutes long. That tradition is supremely embodied in Sergei Rachmaninov's *Vespers*, which contains a setting of the *Ave Maria*—'Bogoroditse Devo'. This slightly longer setting by Rachmaninov (1873–1943) is probably one of the most sublime pieces of choral music ever written, with its gentle altered ending, using the words 'you have given birth to the Saviour of our souls'.

Music is a great leveller and a means by which opposing views can be reconciled, and to a certain extent the famous and gorgeous setting by Charles Gounod (1818–93) embodies this truth. Often the work is described as being by Bach/Gounod, because the piece that Gounod composed in 1853, entitled *'Méditation sur le 1er prélude de J.S. Bach'*, was exactly that—a melodic meditation written 'above' the first of Bach's *Twenty-Four Preludes and Fugues* for key-board (known as *The Well-tempered Clavier*), which the great German composer wrote in 1722. The first of these preludes, in C major, consists of a simple but inspired set of chord progressions, fanned out as arpeggios, giving a fluid effect, as if bearing us on a journey. Gounod, inspired by this simple beauty, added the prayer to Mary, fitting the Latin text to sustained notes that float and linger in the ethereal spaces created above Bach's watery harmonic structure. The resulting soprano solo is now a staple favourite for weddings worldwide.

Bach, who was a committed German Lutheran, composed the *St Matthew Passion* and cantatas for every Sunday of the church year (see 'Christmas Oratorio', 31 December, p. 167). Gounod was a devout French Roman Catholic and an expert on the works of Palestrina, and he considered entering the priesthood before settling on a career as organist and composer. His *Ave Maria* must therefore be seen as one of the greatest ecumenical works known to us—an unplanned collaboration between Lutheranism and Catholicism that gave birth to a moving song that continues to inspire and uplift so many, so often. Dare we suppose that Mary herself would have been pleased that, in spite of all the controversy, a setting of the *Ave Maria* has quietly crossed ecclesiological boundaries and given pleasure and inspiration to those in sickness and in health, in sorrow and in joy? I think we might!

Prayer

Creator God, we thank you for the example of faith, commitment and love that you offer to us in the life and witness of Mary. May we, like her, respond to your call and live our lives in your service, seeking always to live in harmony with others, in churches, communities and nations, for the sake of her Son, Jesus Christ our Lord. Amen.

MASTERS IN THIS HALL

And Mary said,

'My soul magnifies the Lord,
and my spirit rejoices in God my Saviour,
for he has looked with favour on the lowliness of his servant.
Surely, from now on all generations will call me blessed;
for the Mighty One has done great things for me,
and holy is his name.
His mercy is for those who fear him
from generation to generation.
He has shown strength with his arm;
he has scattered the proud in the thoughts of their hearts.
He has brought down the powerful from their thrones,
and lifted up the lowly;
he has filled the hungry with good things,
and sent the rich away empty.
He has helped his servant Israel,
in remembrance of his mercy,
according to the promise he made to our ancestors,
to Abraham and to his descendants for ever.'

LUKE 1:46–55

Masters in this hall
Hear ye news today,
Brought from over seas
And ever you I pray.

Noel, Noel, Noel
Noel sing we clear!
Holpen all the folk on earth
Born the Son of God so dear!
Noel, Noel,
Noel sing we loud
God to day hath poor folk raised and cast a-down the proud.

Going o'er the hills,
Through the milk-white snow,
Heard I ewes bleat
While the wind did blow.
Noel, Noel, Noel...

Shepherds many an one
Sat among the sheep,
No man spake more word
Than they had been asleep.
Noel, Noel, Noel...

Quoth I, 'Fellows mine,
Why this guise sit ye?
Making but dull cheer,
Shepherds though ye be?'
Noel, Noel, Noel...

Shepherds should of right
Leap and dance and sing,
Thus to see ye sit,
Is a right strange thing'.
Noel, Noel, Noel...

Quoth these fellows then,
'To Bethlem town we go,
To see a mighty lord
Lie in manger low'.
Noel, Noel, Noel…

'How name ye this lord,
Shepherds?' then said I.
'Very God,' they said,
'Come from Heaven high'.
Noel, Noel, Noel…

This is Christ the Lord,
Masters be ye glad!
Christmas is come in,
And no folk should be sad.
Noel, Noel, Noel…

WORDS: WILLIAM MORRIS (1834–96)
MUSIC: FRENCH TRADITIONAL

The words of this rather quaint-sounding carol are not as old as they appear. The man who wrote them is famous for his artistic designs, his wallpaper, his political views, his prose and poetry, but his small contribution to the Christmas carol repertoire has been largely overlooked. For the author of this carol is in fact *the* William Morris, the famous social critic, artist and writer of the Victorian age.

He was born in Walthamstow, near London, and his beautifully decorated house there is now a museum worth making the effort to visit. His wealthy family sent him to Exeter College, Oxford, where he met his lifelong friends and collaborators, Edward Burne-Jones, Ford Maddox Brown and Dante Gabriel Rossetti, brother of Christina (see 'In the bleak mid-winter', 30 December, p. 161). They formed the 'Pre-Raphaelite Brotherhood', rejecting the poor-quality manufacture of decorative arts and architecture and seeking to promote handicrafts, which they considered to be artworks.

After Oxford, Morris joined a firm of architects, but in 1861 he founded Morris, Marshall, Faulkner & Co., which became known for its stained glass, examples of which survive in churches throughout Britain. Morris produced some 150 designs, which are known for their distinctive foliage patterns. The firm later became known as Morris and Company, a name still seen on wallpapers and fabrics today. In 1877 he founded the Society for the Protection of Ancient Buildings, and his interest in historic architecture paved the way for the formation of the National Trust in the UK. He also developed an interest in Icelandic myths, and these often informed his poetry and novels. His influence on C.S. Lewis and J.R.R. Tolkien is not to be overlooked: his writings, *The Wood Beyond the World*, *The House of the Wolfings* and *The Roots of the Mountains* can be seen as precursors of the Narnia stories and of the Middle-earth sagas. In 1892, Morris was invited to become Poet Laureate, a position that he declined.

Morris and his daughter May were two of the first British socialists, and one of his better-known works, *News from Nowhere*, is a fictitious account of a socialist society, partly inspired by Thomas More's *Utopia* (1516), a work that Morris admired and for which he wrote an introduction. Morris' journey into socialism had begun with an evangelical faith which he sadly abandoned. Early in life he contemplated becoming a clergyman, but he eventually decided to devote his life to art instead.

His carol 'Masters in this hall' represents a tiny part of his artistic output. It was first published in 1860 in *Nine Ancient and Goodly Carols for the Merry Tide of Christmas*. The tune was suggested by the architect Edmund Sedding (1836–68), who published the volume. Algernon Charles Swinburne (1837–1909), himself the author of the obscure carol 'Thou whose birth on earth', described Morris' carol as 'one of the co-equal three finest... in the language', and so it was also included in A.H. Bullen's *A Christmas Garland; Carols and Poems from the Fifteenth Century to the Present*, published in 1885.

Morris' predilection for all things medieval can clearly be detected in the carol. The language, so admired by Swinburne, is archaic, but it tells that timeless tale of the shepherds travelling to Bethlehem to greet the Christ-child. The text describes a dialogue between narrator and shepherds, interposing a chorus in which we can detect a hint of Morris' socialist leanings: 'Noel sing we loud, God to day hath poor folk raised and cast a-down the proud.' Such sentiments might well appeal to a socialist who believed that we are equal inasmuch as we all need food, clothes, and shelter, and that it must follow that if anyone is not able to satisfy their needs in these respects there is something wrong with society. The gospel, to Morris, was good news to the poor, and this carol emphasizes that aspect in each and every refrain.

The link with Mary's words at the annunciation (the Magnificat) is clear. Mary's song promises a new world order, a new freedom, a new dawn of salvation, peace and joy. She anticipates the 'Gloria' of the shepherds, and Morris' account of meeting the shepherds reminds us of it. For Morris, the 'Masters in this hall' might have been the bourgeois wealthy who need to pay attention to the gospel for the poor and lowly (such as shepherds), perhaps by becoming socialists, in order to promote equality of wealth and resources for all people. Socialism and Christianity are by no means opposed in outlook, and it could be said that the 'official' manifestations of both have had their ups and downs over the years. Worldviews are so often damaged by those who adhere to them.

Quality of workmanship and integrity of politics inspired and drove Morris, and we can only admire his output, his determination, his breadth of life and work. His death at the relatively young age of 62 may have been partly due to the workload he took upon himself, but which yielded a prolific output of art, literature and political involvement. As an advocate of a cause (or three!), he is an example to anyone who seeks to better their world, to bring good news and hope to others, and who always wants to do everything to the best of their ability.

When we consider Mary and her response to the angel's greeting, we have an even greater example to admire. Her words are humble and comforting, but also challenging to all who follow her in the path of faith. Mary's 'yes' to God is a submissive 'yes' but at the same time she takes control and responsibility for the very act of service to which it leads. In her response to Gabriel, Mary identifies and accepts the will of God. She could have said 'no', which means that in choosing to accept, she not only preserves her human freedom but also turns her acquiescence into an almost defiant 'yes' that affirms the poverty and weakness of many, for whom the coming of the Messiah will be a release from captivity. Mary knows this, and she accepts it with joy, gratitude and a certain defiance that has made her words a touchstone for the poor and downtrodden ever since.

Prayer

Mighty God and Father of us all, we rejoice in your salvation by which you bless the world. You look favourably on all who are impoverished in mind, body or spirit, and in your holiness you do great things for your people. Have mercy on all who fear the strength of your arm, and scatter the foolishness of pride, prejudice and power. Fill us instead with good things, according to the promises you have revealed in Jesus Christ, your Son, our Lord. Amen.

THE CHERRY TREE CAROL

Now the birth of Jesus the Messiah took place in this way. When his mother Mary had been engaged to Joseph, but before they lived together, she was found to be with child from the Holy Spirit. Her husband Joseph, being a righteous man and unwilling to expose her to public disgrace, planned to dismiss her quietly. But just when he had resolved to do this, an angel of the Lord appeared to him in a dream and said, 'Joseph, son of David, do not be afraid to take Mary as your wife, for the child conceived in her is from the Holy Spirit. She will bear a son, and you are to name him Jesus, for he will save his people from their sins.' All this took place to fulfil what had been spoken by the Lord through the prophet: 'Look, the virgin shall conceive and bear a son, and they shall name him Emmanuel', which means, 'God is with us.' When Joseph awoke from sleep, he did as the angel of the Lord commanded him; he took her as his wife, but had no marital relations with her until she had borne a son; and he named him Jesus.

MATTHEW 1:18–25

Part One

Joseph was an old man,
And an old man was he,
When he married Mary
In the land of Galilee.

And as they were walking
Through an orchard so good,
Where were cherries and berries
As red as any blood.

O then bespoke Mary,
With words both meek and mild,
'Pluck me one cherry, Joseph,
For that I am with child.'

Go to the tree then Mary,
And it shall bow to thee
And you shall gather cherries
By one, by two, by three.

Then bow'd down the highest tree
Unto our Lady's hand:
'See,' Mary cried, 'See, Joseph,
I have cherries at command!'

'O eat your cherries, Mary,
O eat your cherries now;
O eat your cherries, Mary,
That grow upon the bough.'

Then Mary pluck'd a cherry
As red as any blood;
Mary went she homewards
All with her heavy load.

WORDS AND MUSIC: ENGLISH TRADITIONAL

We know little about Joseph and it is often assumed that he had died by the time Jesus reached maturity. This is why, in the Roman Catholic Church, he is revered as the patron saint of a 'good death'. He is also venerated as the patron of the family and, more recently, as Joseph 'the worker': the carpenter, who laboured at the plane and the lathe, educating his son Jesus in that trade (see Matthew 13:55). In the apocryphal 'protoevangelium' of St James (attributed to him), Joseph is described as old, and some people like the idea that he may have been married before, being the widowed father of other sons, who are described by Matthew as Jesus' brothers James, Joseph, Simon and Judas. While this view accommodates the traditional idea that Mary remained virgin and had no other children, there is little biblical evidence for it—quite the contrary, in fact.

We do know that Joseph was a decent man whose engagement to Mary had been properly made. This meant that although she was still living with her parents, they were legally bound, such that if he had died in that period, she would have become a widow. Sex was not permitted before marriage, so she should not have been pregnant. Given that she was, Joseph would have known that she could be stoned, but also that the custom at that time would be to divorce her. He could do this publicly, by demanding a trial, and since he was a righteous or law-abiding citizen, his contemporaries might have expected him to do so. It is therefore not his righteousness that makes him protect her: a 'righteous' man would have put her on trial.

Joseph not only knows his law, being a righteous man, but he also knows his scripture. When the angel quotes from Isaiah 7:14, it is a reminder to him. It is as though the angel is saying, 'Joseph, don't worry. You remember the old prophecy about a virgin conceiving and a Messiah being born? Well, this is it!' Joseph does not do as he is told merely because an angel tells him to, but because he knows the score: it is revealed to him how he fits in and what is going on in the divine plan. It is, then, no surprise that he does as he is commanded and marries Mary.

Given what his contemporaries expected him to do, Joseph is courageous. He is risking a scandal, not so much because others might suspect that he is not Jesus' father, but because they would assume that he is, and that intercourse had taken place before marriage. This is why Matthew specifically tells us that no such thing happened. Matthew not only emphasizes the miraculous nature of Jesus' conception, he also protects Joseph's honour in the event of future doubt. For then, as now, people are prone to gossip, to draw conclusions from half-facts and casual acquaintance. Thus reputations are ruined and falsehoods spread. Fortunately, Matthew is clear and precise as he reveals the truth of Jesus' birth.

The medieval carol that tells the story of Joseph's dilemma appears in various versions and of different lengths. It is helpful to think of it as being in three parts: the first concerns a slightly mythical account of how Mary and Joseph related to one another when she told him she was pregnant; the second part deals with the events of Christmas Eve; and the third part is more Lenten in feel.

There are far too many verses recounting a conversation between Mary and Joseph to reproduce them all here. One verse that is rarely sung touches a harsh note as Joseph criticizes Mary for having got pregnant:

> *O then bespoke Joseph*
> *With words so unkind,*
> *'Let him pluck thee a cherry*
> *That brought thee with child.'*

Joseph repents of his barbed words when the minor miracle of the tree bowing to her occurs. On one level it all seems a bit trivial, but there is a sort of underlying humanity that we can respect, as we are here being given a fictitious glimpse into their relationship. It must be tough being told that your spouse is carrying someone else's child, and Joseph would have undoubtedly gone through some emotional turmoil.

Joseph faces the traditional dilemma between the head and the heart. He follows his heart, and thinks in terms of a quiet divorce, which could be effected with just two witnesses. Significantly, even before he knows the full story, he is not swift to anger or keen to take revenge on his apparently errant wife-to-be. Rather, he seems to be following the dictum of his soon-to-be son: 'I desire mercy, not sacrifice' (Matthew 9:13).

In Joseph, we see a tendency to be merciful in the face of the law—an ability to respond to situations with compassion, consideration and carefulness. It is something that Jesus himself was later to advocate, and it is an approach that is characteristic of Christianity. In a world full of laws and regulations, we should remember Joseph, who knew how to be flexible for the sake of another's good.

Prayer

Heavenly Father, as you sent an angel to Joseph, that his will and yours might be united, fill us with the same courage, compassion and mercy that we find in Joseph, and just as he adopted Jesus as his own, so may we be adopted as your sons and daughters, in the faith and love of Jesus Christ, your Son, our Lord. Amen.

HARK! THE HERALD ANGELS SING

In that region there were shepherds living in the fields, keeping watch over their flock by night. Then an angel of the Lord stood before them, and the glory of the Lord shone around them, and they were terrified. But the angel said to them, 'Do not be afraid; for see—I am bringing you good news of great joy for all the people: to you is born this day in the city of David a Saviour, who is the Messiah, the Lord. This will be a sign for you: you will find a child wrapped in bands of cloth and lying in a manger.' And suddenly there was with the angel a multitude of the heavenly host, praising God and saying, 'Glory to God in the highest heaven, and on earth peace among those whom he favours!'
LUKE 2:8–14

Hark! the herald angels sing
Glory to the newborn King;
Peace on earth and mercy mild,
God and sinners reconciled:
Joyful all ye nations rise,
Join the triumph of the skies,
With the angelic host proclaim,
Christ is born in Bethlehem:
Hark! the herald angels sing
Glory to the new-born King.

Christ, by highest heaven adored,
Christ, the everlasting Lord,
Late in time behold him come,
Offspring of a Virgin's womb!
Veiled in flesh the Godhead see,
Hail the incarnate Deity!
Pleased as man with man to dwell,
Jesus, our Emmanuel:

Hail the heaven-born Prince of Peace!
Hail the Sun of Righteousness!
Light and life to all he brings,
Risen with healing in his wings;
Mild, he lays his glory by,
Born that man no more may die,
Born to raise the sons of earth,
Born to give them second birth:

WORDS: CHARLES WESLEY (1707– 88), GEORGE WHITFIELD (1714–70),
MARTIN MADAN (1726–90) AND WILLIAM HAYMAN CUMMINGS (1831–1915)
MUSIC: MENDELSSOHN, FROM A CHORUS BY FELIX MENDELSSOHN-BARTHOLDY (1809– 47),
ADAPTED BY WILLIAM HAYMAN CUMMINGS

The carol we now know as 'Hark! the herald angels sing' did not start life as such, and required at least four people to bring it to its current form. Wesley's original, written as a Christmas Day hymn and first published in 1739, is made up of ten four-line verses, rather than the longer eight-line verses with refrain which we have now. It began like this:

Hark, how all the welkin rings,
'Glory to the King of kings;
Peace on earth, and mercy mild,
God and sinners reconcil'd!'

Joyful, all ye nations, rise,
Join the triumph of the skies;
Universal nature say,
'Christ the Lord is born to-day!'

'Welkin' is an Old English word that means 'sky' or 'vault of heaven', and is found in Chaucer, Shakespeare and Wordsworth. It is interesting to note that in this original version of Wesley's, the heavens ring with the phrase 'Glory to the King of kings', echoing Luke's 'Glory to God in the highest heaven'. George Whitfield, who had been a student with Wesley, changed this to 'Glory to the new-born King' in 1753 (see also 'Lo! he comes with clouds descending', 4 December, p. 27). His fairly revolutionary Calvinist position was not compatible with Wesley's gentler reforming approach, which eventually bore fruit in the Methodist movement that he and his brother John inspired. Whitfield maintained the four-line verses of Wesley's original, but changed the angels' emphasis: 'Glory to the new-born King' means something slightly but significantly different to 'Glory to the King of kings'. In the Gospel account the angels praise God, whereas in 'Hark! the herald angels sing', they are inaccurately described as praising Jesus. Furthermore, Luke does not say that the angels 'sing', and so it may well be that this reinterpretation by Whitfield has emphasized the popular but unscriptural picture of angels singing the *Gloria*. ('While shepherds watched' also implies that they sang.)

Whitfield also cut the final verses, which are now largely forgotten:

Come, desire of nations, come,
Fix in us thy humble home;
Rise, the woman's conquering seed,
Bruise in us the serpent's head.

Now display thy saving power,
Ruin'd nature now restore;
Now in mystic union join
Thine to ours, and ours to thine.

Adam's likeness, Lord, efface,
Stamp thy image in its place.
Second Adam from above,
Reinstate us in thy love.

Let us thee, though lost, regain,
Thee, the life, the inner man:
O, to all thyself impart,
Form'd in each believing heart.

There is some real theological insight in these neglected verses. First of all we notice the Advent antiphon 'Come, desire of nations, come', followed by a reference to the fall, with the serpent bruising the heel of humanity and Adam bruising its head (Genesis 3:15). Wesley cleverly alters the meaning, asking that the serpent in us (sin) should be bruised (defeated) by Christ, the second Adam, who reinstates us as beloved sons and daughters of God. In the restoration of sinful humanity to a state of grace through the incarnation of Christ, the joining of divine and human nature is also achieved. Consequently, that which was lost (salvation) is gained and a new life is granted to all believers.

The adaptation of the hymn to three eight-line verses was probably done by Charles Burney (1726–1814), an organist and composer who was a friend of Samuel Johnson. His version appeared in 1769, published in Martin Madan's *Lock Collection*. Madan also made a few textual amendments. Any original tune that was used has been largely forgotten, swept away by the popularity of the tune with which the German composer Felix Mendelssohn is credited. It was actually 'discovered' in 1855 by W.H. Cummings, organist of Waltham Abbey, who adapted the melody from Mendelssohn's

Festgesang an die Kunstler ('Festival song for an artist'), first performed at a festival in June 1840 commemorating the achievements of Johannes Gutenberg (1400–68), who is generally acknowledged to have invented printing. His greatest printing achievement was the 'Gutenberg Bible'—the first of many editions of the greatest book in history—in which is contained the account of the word made flesh, and the story of Christ in words. It is fitting that such a great Christmas hymn should have its musical beginnings in a piece praising the man who did so much to make the mass distribution of the Bible possible for future generations.

The tune we now call MENDELSSOHN comes from the second chorus, *'Gott ist Licht'* ('God is Light'). While there can be no doubt that the marriage of Mendelssohn's tune and the adapted words has been most fortuitous, it is rather ironic that Mendelssohn, while recognizing the value of his tune, felt that it would be unsuitable for sacred words. Similarly, Wesley, when writing the original text, suggested that a slow, solemn tune would fit them best. He refused to sing Whitfield's reworking of his words, furious that he had presumed to alter them to suit his own ends. Nowadays, there would probably be an outcry if someone were to suggest even slight changes, and some attempts to 'inclusivize' the language have been coolly received. 'Hark! the herald angels sing' has become part of the institution of Christmas, and while it contains inaccuracies, it also sounds out some wonderful theology, musically reminding us that Jesus, the 'new-born King', is 'Prince of Peace', 'Sun of Righteousness', 'Everlasting Lord', 'Incarnate Deity' and, best of all, 'Emmanuel'—'God with us'. Whatever its creators would have thought about the hymn as it currently stands, it endures not only as a vehicle for mass praise but as a reminder of the great gift that our Father God has given us in his Son Jesus Christ, and which we will celebrate in only a few hours' time.

The hymn reminds us of those words of the angels, 'Glory to God in the highest heaven, and on earth peace among those whom he favours!' (Luke 2:14), which have become the opening lines of the *Gloria in Excelsis Deo* used in communion services all over the world. Although they refer us directly to the good news proclaimed by angels to the shepherds, they have wider significance, for in a sense they sum up the gospel beautifully. God is glorified by them, and this is the object of all our praise and prayer. A vision of heaven is given, reminding us of the eternal hope to which we are called. Yet these words are earthbound, addressing the real condition of our worldly existence and identifying our greatest corporate need and desire: peace. We all have individual wants and difficulties, but as soon as we group ourselves into communities, nations or races, we find that the security and confidence of mutual peace is a constant worry, whether it be peace in our world, in our land, on our streets or in our homes. The shepherds were ordinary people, with very similar needs and hopes to ours. Thus the good news that the angels bring them can be just as comforting and inspiring to us today. Like them, we can rejoice on this night as the angels proclaim anew their eternal message of hope, peace and joy.

Prayer

Glory to you, O Christ, our newborn King! By the light and life which you bring, reconciling sinners, be pleased to fix in us your humble home, so that we too may join the triumph of the skies, where in highest heaven you are adored by saints and angels singing your praises, this holy night and always. Amen.

WHILE SHEPHERDS WATCHED THEIR FLOCKS BY NIGHT

When the angels had left them and gone into heaven, the shepherds said to one another, 'Let us go now to Bethlehem and see this thing that has taken place, which the Lord has made known to us.' So they went with haste and found Mary and Joseph, and the child lying in the manger. When they saw this, they made known what had been told them about this child; and all who heard it were amazed at what the shepherds told them. But Mary treasured all these words and pondered them in her heart. The shepherds returned, glorifying and praising God for all they had heard and seen, as it had been told them.

LUKE 2:15–20

While shepherds watched their flocks by night,
All seated on the ground,
The angel of the Lord came down,
And glory shone around.

'Fear not,' said he (for mighty dread
Had seized their troubled mind),
'Glad tidings of great joy I bring
To you and all mankind.

'To you in David's town this day
Is born of David's line
A Saviour who is Christ the Lord;
And this shall be the sign:

The heavenly Babe you there shall find
To human view displayed,
All meanly wrapped in swathing bands
And in a manger laid.'

Thus spake the Seraph, and forthwith
Appeared a shining throng
Of angels, praising God, who thus
Addressed their joyful song;

'All glory be to God on high,
And to the earth be peace:
Goodwill henceforth from heaven to men
Begin and never cease.'

WORDS: NAHUM TATE (1652–1715)
MUSIC: WINCHESTER OLD, THOMAS ESTE'S PSALTER, 1592; CHRISTMAS, GEORG FRIDERIC
HANDEL (1685–1759); CRANBROOK, THOMAS CLARK (1775– 1859)

Happy Christmas! As is right and proper today, we continue the
reading about the shepherds abiding in the fields, watching their
flocks by night, who are suddenly greeted by the angels in the skies,
offering the first ever rendition of the *Gloria in Excelsis Deo*: 'Glory
to God in the highest!' Anglicans now sing some version or other of
that first Christian outpouring of praise at most Sunday services,
except during Lent and Advent, when it is felt to be too joyful
for such sombre, penitential seasons. Now, when we arrive at
Christmas (or Easter for that matter), the singing of the *Gloria* has
much more impact, because we have not heard or sung it for a
while. All this contributes to the liturgical drama of the season.

The carol is basically a retelling of the Christmas Day Gospel
reading. The words date from around 1700, and are by Nahum Tate,
an Irishman who settled in London in 1672, becoming Poet
Laureate and Historiographer Royal (court historian). He was a
friend of the poet John Dryden, and wrote the libretto for the opera

Dido and Aeneas in 1689, for which Henry Purcell wrote the music. He met a rather sorry end in a debtor's prison, having become an alcoholic, but he was nevertheless buried in the recently completed St Paul's Cathedral in London.

Tate is reckoned to have written 'While shepherds watched' as part of his contribution to a collaborative work with the Reverend Nicholas Brady entitled *New Version of the Psalms of David, Fitted to the Tunes used in Churches*, which was published in 1696. Other well-known hymns from that collection include 'Through all the changing scenes of life' (Psalm 34) and 'As pants the hart' (Psalm 42). 'While shepherds watched' is not a psalm, of course, but a paraphrase, and it found its way into *A Supplement to the New Version of Psalms by Dr Brady and Mr Tate* published in 1700.

The text has been altered slightly in various times and places. A Scottish variant opens 'While humble shepherds watched their flocks', and another version has 'While shepherds watched their fleecy care'. A southern Yorkshire tradition adds a refrain, 'Sweet bells, sweet chiming Christmas bells, they cheer us on our heavenly way', which adds an extra festive dimension.

When it comes to the tune, the situation is even more complicated. There are or have been over a hundred tunes for this carol, and even now the Atlantic is divided by two tunes. WINCHESTER OLD, the tune invariably used in Britain, first appeared in 1592 in *The Whole book of Psalms with their wonted tunes as they are sung in churches*, published by Thomas Este (c. 1540–c.1608), a Londoner who was instrumental in publishing the madrigals of his day. Sometimes the tune is attributed to the 16th-century English composer Christopher Tye, who was master of music at Ely Cathedral. Whether he wrote it or not, the 1861 collection *Hymns Ancient and Modern* cemented the marriage of words and tune now taken for granted in much of England.

In the United States, the tune CHRISTMAS is generally preferred, but is not well known in the UK. It comes from Handel's Italian opera *Siroe, King of Persia* (1728) and was adapted and published in *Harmonia Sacra*, 1812. One of the most interesting tunes for the carol is CRANBROOK by Thomas Clark, a Canterbury man who visited the town of that name (18 miles east of Tunbridge Wells in Kent), and who, with the assistance of a schoolmaster called John Francis, published the tune in 1805 (some editions date it at 1812). In 1877, CRANBROOK was purloined by the Yorkshire Glee Choir and used for the amusing folk song 'On Ilkley Moor baht 'at'. That delightful text runs:

> *Where hast tha been sin' I saw thee, I saw thee?*
> *On Ilkley Moor baht 'at*
> *Where hast tha been sin' I saw thee, I saw thee?*
> *Where hast tha been sin' I saw thee?*
> *On Ilkley Moor baht 'at*
> *On Ilkley Moor baht 'at*
> *On Ilkley Moor baht 'at.*

> *Tha's been a-courtin' Mary Jane…*

> *Tha's boun' to catch thy death of cold…*

> *Then we shall ha' to bury thee…*

> *Then t' worms'll come and eat thee up…*

> *Then ducks'll come and eat up t' worms…*

> *Then we shall go and eat up t' ducks…*

> *Then we shall all ha' eaten thee…*

Those who know this folk song, and are used to WINCHESTER OLD, often find the juxtaposition of the two rather curious, but there is a sense in which singing 'While shepherds watched' to the tune of 'Ilkley Moor' is far from unacceptable!

The very story that the carol tells is also quite strange. Shepherds minding their own business, guarding flocks at night, are bombarded with angelic song from on high, apparently telling them good news that a little baby who has been born in a stable is going to bring about peace and reconciliation. It is not surprising that they were amazed, nor that many since then, and today, find the story so fantastical as to be unbelievable. Yet the story persists, and continues not only to appeal but to strike notes of beauty and chords of truth even into the hearts of cynical 21st-century humanity. The pastoral setting of the story, and the spiritual context of salvation in Christ, are closed books to so many today, yet there is something in the angels' song that we still long for and hope for.

As with the carol, there have been so many interpretations, so many different ways of singing the song of salvation, some of which have been better or more beautiful than others, but through it all the truth persists. 'While shepherds watched their flocks by night' has had so many different incarnations, and has presented so many possibilities, that it can be hard to remember that ultimately it is a song of good news: good news of salvation brought about in the one and only incarnation of Jesus Christ, the Son of God, who took our flesh so that when we 'catch our death', we will not simply be handed back to earth to be eaten by worms and recycled, but will ourselves become caught up in that angelic hymn of praise, offered for the glory of God on earth and in heaven.

Prayer

Glory to you, heavenly Father, for in Christ you have cast away our fear and, by your angels, have brought to us a hope of goodwill among all nations. Keep watch over us, the sheep of your pasture, and lead us into all peace until that day when, with angels and archangels, we will sing your praises in the highest heaven, where you reign, with the Spirit and the Son, Jesus Christ our Lord. Amen.

GOOD KING WENCESLAS

'Then the king will say to those at his right hand, "Come, you that are blessed by my Father, inherit the kingdom prepared for you from the foundation of the world; for I was hungry and you gave me food, I was thirsty and you gave me something to drink, I was a stranger and you welcomed me, I was naked and you gave me clothing, I was sick and you took care of me, I was in prison and you visited me." Then the righteous will answer him, "Lord, when was it that we saw you hungry and gave you food, or thirsty and gave you something to drink? And when was it that we saw you a stranger and welcomed you, or naked and gave you clothing? And when was it that we saw you sick or in prison and visited you?" And the king will answer them, "Truly I tell you, just as you did it to one of the least of these who are members of my family, you did it to me."'

MATTHEW 25:34–40

Good King Wenceslas looked out
On the Feast of Stephen,
When the snow lay round about,
Deep, and crisp, and even:
Brightly shone the moon that night,
Though the frost was cruel,
When a poor man came in sight,
Gathering winter fuel.

'Bring me flesh, and bring me wine,
Bring me pine-logs hither:
Thou and I will see him dine,
When we bear them thither.'

Page and monarch, forth they went,
Forth they went together;
Through the rude wind's wild lament
And the bitter weather.

'Hither, page, and stand by me,
If thou knowest it, telling.
Yonder peasant, who is he?
Where and what his dwelling?'
'Sire, he lives a good league hence,
Underneath the mountain,
Right against the forest fence,
By Saint Agnes' fountain.'

'Sire, the night is darker now,
And the wind blows stronger;
Fails my heart, I know not how;
I can go no longer.'
'Mark my footsteps, good my page;
Tread thou in them boldly:
Thou shalt find the winter's rage
Freeze thy blood less coldly.'

In his master's steps he trod,
Where the snow lay dinted;
Heat was in the very sod
Which the Saint had printed.
Therefore, Christian men, be sure,
Wealth or rank possessing,
Ye who now will bless the poor,
Shall yourselves find blessing.

WORDS: JOHN MASON NEALE (1818–66)
MUSIC: FROM *PIAE CANTIONES*, THEODERICI PETRI NYLANDENSIS, 1582

This popular carol was written by the prolific English hymn writer John Mason Neale in 1853. Neale translated many Latin hymns, but this one he wrote specifically as a carol to promote a spirit of generosity. Boxing Day, which is more properly kept as the feast day of Stephen the first Christian martyr, was also the day on which the servants and tradesmen serving a wealthy household would receive a gift from the master or lord. This became known as the Christmas 'box', hence 'Boxing Day'. It is in this context that we must consider 'Good King Wenceslas'.

Neale felt that the Christian virtue of generosity should be promoted, especially at Christmas time, and he was well aware of the power of hymns and carols to influence people's thinking and behaviour. Thus he turned to the old legend of King Wenceslas for a story on which to pin his moral purpose. Before actually writing the words, he chose an appropriate tune from an 16th-century tune book from the Finnish cathedral city of Turku, known as *Piae Cantiones*. The tune he chose was originally allied with a Latin text *'Tempus adest floridium'* ('Spring has unwrapped her flowers'), and some people, among them Ralph Vaughan Williams, have criticized Neale's substitution of what they considered to be 'doggerel' for a perfectly good set of springtime words. Doggerel or not, the text and the popular tune have survived. The words tell a story, and lend themselves to a slightly dramatized rendition, with page and king being sung by soloists or alternately by the men and women present.

In the song, we learn only a little about that good king who went out in bitter weather to help the poor, and encouraged his servant who went with him. In reality, Wenceslas was a prince of Bohemia, in what is now the Czech Republic. His story really begins when his grandmother Ludmilla became a Christian. Wenceslas' pagan mother Drahomira ruled Bohemia at the time; the powerful non-Christians resented Ludmilla's influence, and she was murdered in 921. Wenceslas was then still a prince, but he assumed power in 922 when Drahomira was ousted, and he ruled Bohemia as a Christian. He gained a reputation for being friendly to the German realms that neighboured his own, and promoted good order among his citizens. Popular with the people as this approach may have been, it was not liked by his younger brother, Boleslav. In 929, Boleslav invited Wenceslas to stay with him, and, after a quarrel broke out between them, Boleslav's men killed Wenceslas. Consequently, he and his grandmother Ludmilla are revered as martyrs especially in the region around the Czech Republic, for which he became patron saint. The main square in Prague is still named after him.

While historical evidence is a bit thin, Neale would have us believe that Wenceslas was a good, honest and strongly principled man. The song describes him braving a fierce storm in order to help to feed a hungry neighbour. This practical faith reminds us of the parable of the sheep and the goats, where Jesus very clearly teaches us to look after those in need, to visit the sick and clothe the naked. In Wenceslas' time, there were no doubt many poor, but it is hardly different today. To some extent, the help that the poor and the homeless receive is now better organized, but it is never enough, and organizations such as Shelter and Crisis at Christmas always seem to need more money and volunteers. Wenceslas' example, immortalized in this carol, is certainly one to follow. People still die of cold in their homes and on the streets of our towns and cities in 21st-century Britain, and so we should be generous with our money, our time and our prayers, as we are able.

Although Neale specifically sought to encourage generosity and social responsibility with this carol, it also contains some comfort and encouragement for the Christian pilgrim. As master and page go forward together, we might think of our journey with Christ, and, as in the experience of these two characters, there is sometimes bitter weather to endure. Then we might be reminded of the words of the master to the page: 'hither, page, and stand by me', and his injunction to 'mark my footsteps'. As the well-known hymn by J.E. Bode puts it:

O let me see thy footmarks,
and in them plant mine own;
my hope to follow duly
is in thy strength alone.

Wenceslas and his page boy remind us that we are not alone on our journey, especially if we go out to help others, and that Jesus will not abandon us if we seek to walk in the path of compassion in which he leads us. This journey of faith may well take us into cold, inhospitable, even dangerous places. Wenceslas himself knew this, ultimately suffering martyrdom. As we walk in our master's footsteps, we must be aware that we are walking not only the path of truth and light and love, but also the way of the cross. Jesus himself said to his disciples, 'If any want to become my followers, let them deny themselves and take up their cross daily and follow me' (Luke 9:23).

This is our calling, just as it was for the first disciples and for St Stephen, the first Christian martyr, whose feast day it is today. At Christmas time we celebrate and rejoice over the good news revealed in the crib, but we also remind ourselves of the suffering of the saints in many places throughout history, and we praise God for their example, striving always to be generous in material things and in spirit.

Prayer

Holy Jesus, as we seek always to walk in your footsteps, caring for others and blessing those who are poor in body or in spirit, guide us by the example of your saints, and in the power of your Spirit fill us with compassion and generosity, for you are our friend and master, now and always. Amen.

THE CANDLE SONG

In the beginning was the Word, and the Word was with God, and the Word was God. He was in the beginning with God. All things came into being through him, and without him not one thing came into being. What has come into being in him was life, and the life was the light of all people. The light shines in the darkness, and the darkness did not overcome it.

There was a man sent from God, whose name was John. He came as a witness to testify to the light, so that all might believe through him. He himself was not the light, but he came to testify to the light. The true light, which enlightens everyone, was coming into the world.

JOHN 1:1–9

Like a candle flame,
Flick'ring small
in our darkness.
Uncreated light
shines through infant eyes.

God is with us, alleluia,
God is with us, alleluia,
Come to save us, alleluia,
Come to save us, alleluia.
Alleluia.

Stars and angels sing,
yet the earth
sleeps in shadows;
can this tiny spark
set a world on fire?

Yet his light shall shine
from our lives,
Spirit blazing,
As we touch the flame
of his holy fire.

WORDS AND MUSIC: GRAHAM KENDRICK (B. 1950)

We have become a nation of candle-lighters. As well as the time-honoured practice of lighting birthday candles, candles are now the chic accessories at home, for dinner parties, summer's evenings and winter days. In spite of the other more efficient and cheaper ways of creating light, we are still attracted to the flickering, vulnerable light source that somehow communicates to us the fragility of our own existence. In some European cathedrals, where there has long been a tradition of lighting candles as a form of prayer, recent technology has encouraged the faithful to pay to switch on an electric candle-shaped bulb, which then 'burns' for a predetermined length of time. This (in my opinion) lamentable development in commercialized spirituality has not dampened our desire to light real candles, and indeed, events such as the death of Diana, Princess of Wales in 1997 sparked off (as it were) a new trend in lighting candles as a form of memorial prayer whenever there has been some kind of tragedy.

Candles also feature at vigils of prayer before a major event: we might remember the scenes from East Germany just before the Berlin Wall came down in 1989, with thousands of candles lit as a gesture of hope for a peaceful reunification. At other times, such as after the terrible events of 11 September 2001 or the bombs in Madrid in March 2004, candles are lit almost as an act of defiance, as if to say to the perpetrators of violence, 'You will not extinguish us.' Those small candles, adorning makeshift shrines to the dead and injured, make for an ironic contrast to the big blazes of heat and light that illuminate some of the explosive skies above those places where anger, hatred and revenge burn the core of humanity.

Candles symbolize a prayer, or a wish, a hope for something good, or even a way of handling pain—of burning it away in a tiny blaze of light. Of course, pain and evil cannot simply be burned away with a candle (if only it were so easy!), but lighting one comforts many people. We must also remember the spirituality of the paschal candle, the great Easter candle that symbolizes the light of the risen Christ shining in the midst of the darkness of sin. It burns at baptisms, and a smaller candle, lit from it, is given to the newly baptized. Thus we are baptized not only into Jesus' death but into his resurrection (Romans 6:3–5). At Christmas, when at Bethlehem we welcome the light of the world, it is good to be reminded of the final outcome as God's love blazes from the cross and rises, unextinguished, on the third day. God is with us, yes, and he has come to save us.

The singer and songwriter Graham Kendrick was evidently in touch with this kind of spirituality when he wrote 'The candle song'. The popularity and success of his worship music is a phenomenon to be admired and celebrated. There can be no doubt that the stream of praise that he has unleashed in recent years has touched the hearts of many, and enabled countless others to welcome the Spirit of God into worship and daily life. Songs such as 'Shine, Jesus, shine' will remain popular for many years to come. Kendrick combines tuneful music with straightforward accompaniment, but most of all he imbues his work with an authenticity of praise that strikes chords in those who join with him. His ability to resource today's church is something to be truly grateful for, and many testify to a ministry that transcends his music-making.

He began his musical career at home in London in the 1960s, largely teaching himself. Playing by ear and using guitar chord charts, he began picking up tunes and composing them in his head.

He claims that he saw music in terms of colours ('synaesthesia' is the technical term) and it was a while before he began to write music down in a conventional way. At home he would listen to the Beatles, Pink Floyd and the Rolling Stones, while singing hymns from the *Baptist Hymn Book* in church on Sundays. In due course he began to write lyrics and music himself, which he performed, and his first worship song was called 'Long as I live'. At 22 he sang at an event at which Billy Graham was the speaker, and was surprised and honoured when the great evangelist quoted from one of the songs he had just sung. Kendrick's career took off thereafter, and 'The candle song' was written as part of a festive presentation called *The Gift*, a collection of songs for Christmas.

Writing music today is as much about recording songs as composing them. Sometimes the final version of a song does not take shape until the musicians are gathered in the studio, and changes are made even during the recording sessions. The days of country vicars writing hymns and publishing them privately have given way to recording contracts, deadlines and themed releases. Thus Christmas songs may have to be written in the height of summer, and the song isn't finished until it's been recorded.

'The candle song' was produced with a choir of boys, and, to a certain extent, is the most traditional-sounding of the Christmas songs that Kendrick has written. Using a boy choir evokes cathedral choristers and large spaces, but doing so also reminds us that Jesus himself was a little boy once, born vulnerable and cold, yet to be the light of the world.

Jesus the Son was in the beginning, and was with God, and was God, and is God. He came into the same world that his Father created, like a candle burning in a pitch-dark cave, but the glare of mercy was too much for many, who rejected him. Yet there are others who, then and now, recognize the light of God burning in Christ through the ages. This is the light of Christ begun with a little spark, setting the world on fire: Christ the same yesterday and today, the light shining from our lives in a blaze of glory, illuminating the gift of eternal, resurrection life. God is with us, Alleluia!

Prayer

God with us, God among us, God within us, shine from our lives with the glow of joy that filled your fatherly heart when your Son came into the world. As your heavenly light took human form and shone through the eyes of the baby Jesus, shine the light of your love through the dark glass of our vision, so that your word may always be a lamp to our feet and a light on our path. Amen.

THE COVENTRY CAROL

When Herod saw that he had been tricked by the wise men, he was infuriated, and he sent and killed all the children in and around Bethlehem who were two years old or under, according to the time that he had learned from the wise men. Then was fulfilled what had been spoken through the prophet Jeremiah: 'A voice was heard in Ramah, wailing and loud lamentation, Rachel weeping for her children; she refused to be consoled, because they are no more.'

MATTHEW 2:16–18

> *Lullay, Thou little tiny Child,*
> *By, by, lully, lullay.*
> *Lullay, Thou little tiny Child,*
> *By, by, lully, lullay.*
>
> *O sisters too, how may we do,*
> *For to preserve this day.*
> *This poor youngling for whom we sing*
> *By, by, lully, lullay.*
>
> *Herod the king, in his raging,*
> *Charged he hath this day.*
> *His men of might, in his own sight,*
> *All young children to slay.*

That woe is me, poor Child for Thee!
And ever morn and day,
For thy parting neither say nor sing,
By, by, lully, lullay.

WORDS: FROM THE 'PAGEANT OF THE SHEARMEN AND TAYLORS' (15TH CENTURY), POSSIBLY
ANNOTATED BY ROBERT CROO AND LATER BY THOMAS SHARP, 1817, FROM *DISSERTATION ON THE
PAGEANTS OR DRAMATIC MYSTERIES ANCIENTLY PERFORMED AT COVENTRY*, 1825
MUSIC: ANONYMOUS, 1591

The dramatic and emotionally engaging story of Herod's killing of
the children is one that cannot fail to touch the heart of anyone who
hears it. On this day, the church remembers those poor children—
the holy innocents. It is often said that no matter how much we
might disagree on some moral issues, there is no reasonable society
that tolerates the torture of children. Yet it happens, often because
adults are frightened of the children who are destined to follow
them. Herod killed because these little babies were a threat to him,
not because of who they were but because of what he feared one of
them might become—a rival. Thus we must honour these poor
children, for they, unwittingly, died in Christ's place. Jesus was the
intended victim, but he escaped to Egypt with Mary and Joseph. He
survived and became the man born to die as a victim for all of us,
but not at that time and place, so soon after being revealed to the
world. Thus by divine providence he was saved, and by human evil
others were brutally and tragically murdered.

We have seen too many cases of parents who can't cope with
their children, who resent them, and who abuse or kill them, acci-
dentally, negligently, sometimes wilfully. The names of Ian Huntley,
Ian Brady, Myra Hindley and Thomas Hamilton have all become
notorious on the roll of child-killers in recent years, and no one will
ever forget the school in Beslan, Russia, which witnessed a terrorists'
massacre of the innocents in September 2004. Aberrant and unusual as child-killing is, it is sadly not unique or even especially rare.

It is to the heritage of English literature that we look to cast some
light on the famous and ancient Coventry Carol. Both the music

and the text are from the 'Pageant of the Shearmen and Taylors', a medieval mystery play from the set of plays that were regularly performed in that city. Mystery plays date back at least as far as the great English poet Geoffrey Chaucer, who died in 1400. His *Canterbury Tales*, while not mystery plays as such, owe a great deal to that tradition, whereby religious subjects and fables are blended together to create a mixture of entertainment and moral teaching.

Medieval literature and drama grew out of church devotion, and while mystery plays were often performed in the street, their material was invariably biblical in origin. Their main purpose was to bring the Bible alive to a population that enjoyed pageantry and could not read the texts for themselves. The English word 'mystery' is derived from the French word *métier*, meaning 'trade', and London Livery Companies still use the word 'mystery' today. In the 1501 charter of the Worshipful Company of Coopers, for example, they are referred to as 'the Mistery of Coopers'. In Coventry, as elsewhere, it was often the trade guilds who would present a play, hence the surviving remains of the pageant of Shearmen and Taylors, who combined for such a dramatic purpose. Their pageant told the story of Christ's birth and childhood, beginning with the annunciation (Luke 1) and concluding with the massacre of the Holy Innocents. In the cycle of plays, it was immediately followed by the Weavers' guild production, as they would act out the story of the purification of Mary, the presentation of Christ in the temple (Candlemas) and the story of the young Jesus with the teachers (Luke 2:41–50).

Such events feature liturgically during the season of Epiphany, after Christmas. Manuscripts exist for the Weavers' pageant, but not for the Shearmen and Taylors', which was destroyed when the Birmingham Free Reference Library burned down in 1879. Fortunately, Thomas Sharp, a local antiquarian expert, had transcribed it in 1817, and published it in 1825. The Weavers' manuscript, with Robert Croo's name on it, dates from 1535. This is not to credit Croo with having composed the material, but only with having written it down.

The Shearmen and Taylors' play includes this most tragic and brutal story, which, as we can imagine, lent itself to a certain dramatic effect on stage. Chaucer's Absolon in 'The Miller's Tale' describes himself as an actor in such a play:

> *Sometyme, to shew his lightnesse and maistyre*
> *He playeth Herodes on a scaffold hye.*

The 'scaffold' had nothing to do with executions, but was a temporary stage, sometimes even a cart, on which the drama would be enacted. Being outdoors, and given in the vernacular, the opportunity for extensive, even blasphemous elaboration on the plot, was possible. The furious Herod, demanding the deaths of the infants, would be portrayed in an exaggerated way, no doubt employing colourful language not fit for church!

The Coventry mystery cycle was one of the best-known and drew crowds (including the royal family) from all over the country to watch the series of ten plays that made up the cycle. They were usually performed at Corpus Christi-tide, in the weeks after Trinity Sunday. Summer weather and longer days therefore made it possible to see the whole set in one day.

Usually, a mystery play dealt with a single subject, such as the passion of Christ, or the harrowing of hell. This Coventry Shearmen and Taylors' pageant was more linear in structure, recounting a series of events in dramatic and rapid sequence. Joseph, husband of Mary, is portrayed as an irritable type, who dreads his call to parenthood. He becomes a butt of some of the comedy, a foil to the ever-practical Mary. Herod is seen as the 'chief captain of hell', and there can be little doubt as to how the audience reacted to him. In these mystery plays lie the origins of pantomime and opera. Additional characters include the mothers whose children are slaughtered, and the soldiers who carry out the foul deed.

We should never forget that just as we can think of current examples of this kind of barbarous behaviour, so too could our 16th-century predecessors. In France, Huguenot Protestants in Paris were shot, drowned, hanged and butchered by fanatical Catholics. They were hunted down and killed, and women and children were stripped, dragged through the streets and thrown into the Seine. A basketful of babies was also thrown into the river, and pregnant women had their throats cut. This was on St Bartholemew's Day, 1572, fifty years after Robert Croo annotated the Coventry plays.

Whichever century we look into, including our own, we find that the names and circumstances change, but the scenario does not. We live in a violent, cruel world in which human beings damage, maim and kill one another with calculated spite or mindless violence. This is our world, and it is God's world. It is the same world into which God himself was born, and is only different today because Christ took human flesh and made a difference. He shows us another way, speaking words of comfort and hope to those many who remain wholly innocent of the terrible crimes committed against them either in God's name, or in direct challenge to his ways of light and peace.

Prayer

Father of the old and of the young, hear the cries of your children who wail for your mercy and judgment. Turn the hearts of the cruel and the selfish, and banish all fear of difference, race and creed from our world. Where innocence is drowned and love blemished, shed the healing light of your salvation among friends and foes alike, for the sake of Jesus your beloved Son. Amen.

THE CHILDHOOD OF CHRIST

Now after they had left, an angel of the Lord appeared to Joseph in a dream and said, 'Get up, take the child and his mother, and flee to Egypt, and remain there until I tell you; for Herod is about to search for the child, to destroy him.' Then Joseph got up, took the child and his mother by night, and went to Egypt, and remained there until the death of Herod. This was to fulfil what had been spoken by the Lord through the prophet, 'Out of Egypt I have called my son.'

MATTHEW 2:13–15

Thou must leave thy lowly dwelling,
The humble crib, the stable bare,
Babe, all mortal babes excelling,
Content our earthly lot to share,
Loving father, loving mother,
Shelter thee with tender care!
Loving father, loving mother,
Shelter thee with tender care,
Shelter thee with tender care!

Blessed Jesus, we implore thee
With humble love and holy fear,
In the land that lies before thee,
Forget not us who linger here!
May the shepherd's lowly calling
Ever to thy heart be dear!

May the shepherd's lowly calling
Ever to thy heart be dear,
Ever to thy heart be dear!

Blest are ye beyond all measure,
Thou happy father, mother mild!
Guard ye well your heavn'ly treasure,
The Prince of Peace, the Holy Child!
God go with you, God protect you,
Guide you safely through the wild!
God go with you, God protect you,
Guide you safely through the wild,
Guide you safely through the wild!

WORDS AND MUSIC: HECTOR BERLIOZ (1803–69). TEXT TRANS. PAUL ENGLAND

The story of the temporary exile of the holy family inspired Hector Berlioz' 'Sacred Trilogy', *L'enfance du Christ* (*The Childhood of Christ*), which was first performed at the St Eustache Church in Paris in 1854. It is an unusual work, because it does not conform to the structures of oratorio or opera, and yet it is dramatic and narrative throughout. Berlioz wrote the text as well as the music, creating a set of three portraits or *tableaux* (hence a sacred trilogy). He suggested that the three sections of the piece were like pages of an illuminated medieval manuscript, representing Herod's dream, the flight to Egypt and the arrival at Sais in Egypt.

The first part, 'Herod's Dream', opens with a narrator setting the scene, who reminds us that no sooner had Jesus been born than Herod was plotting a terrible crime, but Jesus' parents would be warned, even while they waited in their humble stable. The action begins with two soldiers, one of whom is called Polydorus. His job is to guard Herod, who is tormented by dreams of treachery. Then we meet Herod, who is so jumpy that he draws his sword. Polydorus informs him that some soothsayers have arrived, and they proceed to offer him loyal service and advice. Herod recounts his fears: 'A child has been recently born who will overthrow your throne and power...' The soothsayers then perform a series of cabbalistic rituals, communing with the spirits of the dead. Consequently they inform Herod that his voices are accurate: a child has indeed been born who will abolish his throne, but no one knows who it is. Thus they advise him to kill all newborn babies. Rather like Macbeth under the influence of witchcraft, Herod is instantly persuaded by evil logic, and he resolves to shed 'rivers of blood'. He will show no pity, nor feel remorse in allaying his own personal fears. Thus the infants of Jerusalem, Nazareth and Bethlehem will fall to the sword.

Berlioz likened his work to that of the medieval manuscript illuminators, and we might also remember that although the scenes with Herod and the soothsayers were written hundreds of years after the medieval plays, they seem to have been influenced by them, as indeed they are by Berlioz' passion for Shakespeare.

The action moves to Bethlehem, where the young Jesus is portrayed feeding the lambs and scattering flowers on their straw, encouraged by his parents. Their idyll is interrupted by the arrival of angels who warn Mary and Joseph that they must flee to Egypt immediately. Mary and Joseph, both used to following the advice of angels, agree, asking them for strength and protection. The angels depart, singing 'Hosanna'.

The central tableau describes the flight to Egypt, opening with an overture and the delightful 'Shepherds' Farewell', which is often heard on its own at carol services and concerts at Christmas-time. The holy family set off on their journey, and they rest by a spring of water. The narrator describes the scene of grass and flowers (in the middle of the desert!), and how the angels worship the Christ-child as he sleeps in the shade. The scene might remind us of Genesis 21:19, the story of mother and son Hagar and Ishmael, who are saved by a similarly miraculous springing up of water in the desert. Here the brief scene ends with angels singing 'Alleluia'.

The third and final part sees Mary, Joseph and Jesus arrive at the ancient Egyptian city of Sais. Archaeologists say that it was in the western Egyptian delta, where there is still a village called Sa el-Hagar, a name which combines the ancient Egyptian name for the city ('Sa') with the Arabic word for 'stone'. This suggests that there was once an impressive city there with many stone buildings. There is no biblical warrant for assuming that the family went to this Roman-occupied city, but the assumption is not so far-fetched. Berlioz's account of their arrival, exhausted, is moving and imaginative. The donkey has died in the desert, and they would not have survived, says the narrator, unless God had given them strength. The locals are not welcoming, however, which causes them further anguish.

Joseph knocks on the door of a house, seeking help, refuge and rest, yet, with words that are often delivered to homeless people today, Joseph is told that he is not wanted. 'Away with you,' the residents say. Mary has bleeding feet, and no more milk, but they are similarly turned away elsewhere. Here is a foretaste of rejections that Jesus will experience in later life (Luke 9:51–55). Eventually they come to the home of an Ishmaelite, who is kind and admits them, and, rather like the good Samaritan (Luke 10:25–37), puts all his resources at their disposal. Their feet are bathed (which reminds us of John 13:2–12) and food and comfort are provided. The Ishmaelite man tells them that the children of Ishmael are brothers to the Israelites, a phrase that resonates today as Christians, Jews and Muslims alike strive to live together, sharing a common heritage but with different beliefs and traditions. If Berlioz, who would not have called himself a Christian, intended anything significant by these words of the Ishmaelite host, he soon moves on to more mundane pleasantries. The host declares that Jesus will be able to grow up in his house and will be useful to Joseph too. The Chorus take up this sentiment, and they all prepare to play music together. What follows is a delightful trio for two flutes and harp, which makes Mary weep with joy. The holy family can at last sleep safely and peacefully, happy in what will be their new home.

Thus, says the narrator, an unbeliever saved Jesus' life, and he tells us that he stayed there for ten years. Then, having developed a sublime, sweet, wise and tender character, Jesus and his family returned to Nazareth, which he left to make the perfect sacrifice that saved humanity and opened the way to salvation. The Chorus conclude the story with an injunction to us all: what more can we do in the light of such a mystery than to be filled with the pure love that opens for us the gate of heaven?

Flight and return are key biblical themes: in the Old Testament the Israelites flee Egypt, where they had previously been secure, and much of their subsequent history is concerned with the hope of a return to a 'promised land'. Much later, there was to be exile in Babylon, and then the return of a remnant. It is ironic, but fitting therefore, that even the young Jesus must also experience the disturbance of exile and eventual return. Just as the Israelites fled from Egypt, so Jesus flees from Israel to Egypt, reversing the order of release and redemption.

Jesus was effectively homeless for a while, a fact that we might expect to have had a bearing on his later life. From an early age, the Son of Man had nowhere to lay his head (see Matthew 8:20), and from this we are also reminded that, like Christ, 'we have no lasting city, but we are looking for the city that is to come' (Hebrews 13:14). We are all rootless without God, and, even as his followers, we wander on our pilgrimage until we reach our heavenly home.

Prayer

Father God, as we remember the poverty and defencelessness of your beloved holy family, feed us with the truth of your gospel and the power of your Spirit, that we may be ever vigilant for the homeless, the abandoned and the destitute, so that all your children may live with dignity and hope until your kingdom come. Amen.

30 December

IN THE BLEAK MID-WINTER

Let the same mind be in you that was in Christ Jesus, who, though he was in the form of God, did not regard equality with God as something to be exploited, but emptied himself, taking the form of a slave, being born in human likeness. And being found in human form, he humbled himself and became obedient to the point of death—even death on a cross. Therefore God also highly exalted him and gave him the name that is above every name, so that at the name of Jesus every knee should bend, in heaven and on earth and under the earth, and every tongue should confess that Jesus Christ is Lord, to the glory of God the Father.

PHILIPPIANS 2:5–11

In the bleak mid-winter
Frosty wind made moan,
Earth stood hard as iron,
Water like a stone;
Snow had fallen, snow on snow,
Snow on snow,
In the bleak mid-winter,
Long ago.

Our God, heav'n cannot hold him
Nor earth sustain;
Heaven and earth shall flee away
When he comes to reign:

In the bleak mid-winter
A stable-place sufficed
The Lord God Almighty,
Jesus Christ.

Enough for him, whom Cherubim
Worship night and day,
A breastful of milk,
And a mangerful of hay:
Enough for him, whom angels
Fall down before,
The ox and ass and camel
Which adore.

Angels and archangels
May have gathered there,
Cherubim and Seraphim
Thronged the air;
But only his mother
In her maiden bliss
Worshipped the Beloved
With a kiss.

What can I give him,
Poor as I am?
If I were a shepherd
I would bring a lamb;
If I were a wise man
I would do my part;
Yet what I can I give him,
Give my heart.

WORDS: CHRISTINA ROSSETTI (1830–94)
MUSIC: CRANHAM, GUSTAV HOLST (1874–1934)

Christina Rossetti was from a well-known literary and artistic family. Her father, Gabriele Rossetti, was a political exile from Naples, who arrived in London in 1825 and ended up as professor of Italian at King's College, London. Christina and her sister Maria were educated at home, where their enlightened parents encouraged the discussion of poetry, religion and politics. Their churchmanship was High Anglican, and they were much inspired by the Tractarianism of the Oxford Movement. (Tractarians were High Church Anglicans who resisted liberalism and sought to promote the succession of priesthood as dating back to the apostles, always affirming the values espoused in the 1662 Prayer Book.)

Tractarianism is not to be confused with Roman Catholicism, and Christina was to be made acutely aware of the gulf between the two when her fiancé James Collinson, a painter, became a Roman Catholic. With her brothers Dante Gabriel Rossetti and William Michael Rossetti, he was among the founders of the Pre-Raphaelite Brotherhood, which gave birth to the 19th-century English art movement of the same name. But when Collinson became a Roman Catholic, Christina broke off the engagement, and consequently never married. Along with her strong faith, expressed in devotional poetry, can also be identified a melancholic atmosphere of unrequited love and longing.

To some extent, Christina was overshadowed in her own time by her brothers' paintings and writings. Only a few of her poems were published in her lifetime, and 'In the bleak mid-winter' had a humble origin which today seems strangely fitting, since, like the Christ-child she describes, a humble beginning can lead to international fame and glory. If Christina Rossetti is famous for one thing, it is probably this carol.

She wrote it in 1872 in response to a request from a magazine called *Scribner's Monthly* for a Christmas poem. The poem did not find its way into any hymn book until after her death, being first published in *The English Hymnal* in 1906, in which Gustav Holst's hauntingly melancholic tune was paired with it. Christina Rossetti probably never heard this carol sung, neither to Holst's tune nor to a tune composed by Harold Darke (1888–1976) in 1911. This later version is set for soloists with choral and organ accompaniment, and captures a very similar flavour of gentleness and awe, especially in the last verse where the choir are intended to evoke a chorus of quietly humming angels. In liturgical use, the carol serves very well indeed as an offertory hymn at a midnight or Christmas Day communion service, because of its clear evocations of Christ's humility and offering of himself, contrasted with the response we might make: 'All things come from God, and of his own do we give him.'

Rossetti's words have a piety and sweetness to them that always appeal at Christmas, but they also express some crucial truths about the birth of our Lord. She speaks of a bleak midwinter, and as we are often told that many people die over the Christmas period because of the cold, it is very easy for us to have a sense of what she means. And yet, the bleakness of the midwinter can have a spiritual meaning too, for it was to a cold, hard earth that Christ came, to be met with coldness of heart and rejection throughout his life before finally being executed on a cross.

The second verse indicates Christ's submission to earthly life in order to be born in that filthy, cold stable. Heaven cannot hold him, because God is bursting to redeem us; yet earth, the domain of sin, could not hold him, preferring to reject him: 'He was despised and rejected by others; a man of suffering and acquainted with infirmity; and as one from whom others hide their faces he was despised, and we held him of no account' (Isaiah 53:3). There is irony in the fact that when Christ returns to reign, both heaven and earth will be subsumed in a new heaven and earth (Revelation 21:1–7). For now, though, as Christ is born among us, a dingy stable will do.

Only the most basic of human needs was met in that stable: a bed of hay and mother's milk. Christ's humility is revealed in the fact that as the firstborn of creation (Colossians 1:15), worshipped in heaven by angels and on earth only by beasts of burden, he took our flesh in conditions that even the people of his own day would have considered too lowly (Philippians 2:5–8).

We must not forget the activity of that most important human being in our Lord's life: his mother Mary. Divinity and humanity are nicely contrasted and combined in the fourth verse as Rossetti tells us that even though all the angels of heaven may have turned up to witness and pay homage at Christ's birth, there was one human being, Mary, who uniquely adored her child in that most tender of ways. Sweet, even over-romanticized as this image may be for some, it does remind us of the contrast between ethereal spirituality and physical humanity, which were brought together in that stable and for the next 30 years or so. Heavenly bodies don't kiss people, but real, loving human beings do.

That stable might remind us of the world in which we live, then and now—a filthy, cold, hard-hearted place. But we can also detect some physical warmth, in human love and basic creature comforts. Because of that very birth, warmth of heart and cleanliness from sin has come into the world, so much that even now, two millennia later, Christ's birth is still associated with generosity, good will and rejoicing. Thus, as we reach the last verse, we find the heart of the matter, and an acknowledgment that God's gift of Christ to us demands a response: 'What can I give him, poor as I am?'

The poverty here is not financial, but spiritual. 'Blessed are the poor in spirit,' Jesus was later to say, 'for theirs is the kingdom of heaven' (Matthew 5:3). We are all poor in spirit, so we can all be blessed.

If I were a shepherd, I would bring a lamb;
If I were a wise man, I would do my part.

Well, that's as may be: would we have brought a gift, had we known? What would we have done in this situation? Would we have humbled ourselves and taken a chance on looking foolish? Would we have had the simple generosity of heart to bring a gift to an unknown newborn baby, if we had been passing by?

Well, what we can say, with Christina Rossetti, is this: 'What I can I give him—give my heart.' We can say it, or even sing it. But can we do it? Can we give ourselves to Jesus? In this question is to be found the meaning of Christmas, and also the challenge of Christmas.

Prayer

Poor as we are, O God, we offer you ourselves. Make of us what you will; use us to your glory. Humble us, exalt us, fill us, deprive us, only let us play our part in the hastening of your kingdom, so that when you come to reign, Father, Son and Holy Spirit, our hearts may suffice as offerings to you. Amen.

CHRISTMAS ORATORIO

Long ago God spoke to our ancestors in many and various ways by the prophets, but in these last days he has spoken to us by a Son, whom he appointed heir of all things, through whom he also created the world. He is the reflection of God's glory and the exact imprint of God's very being, and he sustains all things by his powerful word. When he had made purification for sins, he sat down at the right hand of the Majesty on high, having become as much superior to angels as the name he has inherited is more excellent than theirs. For to which of the angels did God ever say, 'You are my Son; today I have begotten you'? Or again, 'I will be his Father, and he will be my Son'? And again, when he brings the firstborn into the world, he says, 'Let all God's angels worship him.'

HEBREWS 1:1–6

> *Come then, only your name will be in my heart!*
> *Thus I will call upon you, filled with delight,*
> *When heart and breast burn for love of you.*
> *But, my beloved, tell me,*
> *How do I praise you, how do I thank you?*

> *Jesus, my joy and bliss, my hope, treasure and reward,*
> *My redeemer, defence and salvation,*
> *Shepherd and King, light and sun!*
> *Ah! How can I offer you worthy praise, my Lord Jesus?*

WORDS: ATTRIBUTED TO CHRISTIAN FRIEDRICH HENRICI (ALSO KNOWN AS PICANDER) (1700–64)
MUSIC: J.S. BACH (1685–1750)

Many people regard the German composer Johann Sebastian Bach as the greatest composer of sacred music, and we should not overlook him in this book. The main reason that there is so much religious music by Bach is that he spent his working life writing music for liturgical services, first in Weimar, then Cothen and finally as *Kantor* (Cantor—a senior musical post) of St Thomas, Leipzig, where he was appointed in May 1723 and stayed until his death in 1750. The job involved teaching Latin and music at the church school, playing the organ, training the choir, hiring orchestral players and singers and composing music for worship. His *Passions*, written while in Leipzig, are well-known and justifiably famous extended treatments of the passion narratives of St John, St Matthew and St Mark (long lost, but recently recreated), but there were other oratorios, and cantatas for each Sunday of the year, including Easter, Ascension and Christmastide.

The oratorios are basically collections of cantatas, such that the *Christmas Oratorio* is actually a joining together of the cantatas that the 50-year-old Bach composed in 1734, for the period between Christmas and Epiphany 1734–35. Thus there are six cantatas in all—for the first, second and third days after Christmas, for the feast of the circumcision (the naming of Jesus, 1 January), the first Sunday after Christmas, and Epiphany. The performances of these cantatas were shared between the two churches, and Bach never intended or expected them all to be performed on one occasion. Even today it is quite rare to hear performances of the whole of the *Christmas Oratorio*.

Unusually, some of the music we find in the *Christmas Oratorio* Bach lifted from his earlier compositions, perhaps because he had little time. At least eleven musical sections seem to have originated in earlier, secular cantatas, with the music being adapted to new texts. Other parts may also be based on sacred works that have since been lost, such as the *St Mark Passion*. These 'borrowings' are known as 'parodies', and the *Christmas Oratorio* is full of them, although all of the recitatives and chorales appear to have been composed specially.

Each of the six cantatas opens with a chorus or sinfonia (instrumental piece), serving as a call to worship. The second section in each case is a setting of the appointed biblical text, sung by the character of the Evangelist (Gospel writer). The dramatic feel of each cantata is created by soloists tackling the various roles of the key characters, such as the Angel in Part II and Herod in Part VI. The choir contribute by singing the parts of the heavenly host in 'Glory to God' in Part II, the shepherds in 'Let us, even now, go to Bethlehem' in Part III, and the Magi in 'Where is this new-born child; the King of the Jews?' in Part V. Such an approach is very similar to that taken by Bach in his Passions, or indeed by Handel in his *Messiah*.

The text for the day, concerning the shepherds, Herod or the presentation of Christ, forms a sort of keynote from which all else follows. The choruses, chorales and arias that make up the rest of these cantatas are biblical reflections dramatized musically. Thus, in the fourth cantata (Part IV), the text is Luke 2:21: 'After eight days had passed, it was time to circumcise the child; and he was called Jesus, the name given by the angel before he was conceived in the womb.' It is preceded by a chorus in which we are entreated to 'fall down with praise' and followed by a prayer of adoration, sung by a bass soloist:

> *Emmanuel, oh sweet word!*
> *My Jesus is my shepherd,*
> *My Jesus is my life.*
> *My Jesus has given himself to me,*
> *My Jesus will always*
> *Hover in my sight.*
> *My Jesus is my joy,*
> *My Jesus restores heart and breast.*

A chorus of women join in, singing of Christ as their bridegroom who gave himself on the cross. This leads the bass soloist to reflect on the meaning of Christ's passion, acknowledging that because of

Christ's death he will not perish: '... your name, which overcomes the fear of death, is inscribed within me.' A soprano soloist picks up on the possibility of there being even a tiny speck of fear in the face of death, and goes on to exhibit a faith that denies even this possibility: 'Shall I then fear death? No, your sweet name is there,' she sings. The key to these reflections is the name of Jesus, a theme borrowed from the spiritual content of the first day of the year, which we celebrate tomorrow. The message in this cantata is that if we have the name of Jesus inscribed in our hearts, then we shall have no need to fear death: the name of Jesus is the name of our saviour. Yet there is more, for the name of Jesus not only casts out fear, it inspires love and happiness.

This fourth part of the *Christmas Oratorio* concludes with a tenor aria in which the soloist seeks strength to praise Jesus, and then there follows a final chorale. Chorales were introduced into church services by Martin Luther (1483–1546) to enable the congregation to take part in and engage with music in worship. Chorales are rather like hymns: their straightforward tunes were harmonized by the choir or organ, and Bach's congregations would have learnt and sung the chorales that he used in the *Christmas Oratorio* (they were given the texts to follow). Sometimes a chorale melody is used in other movements, elaborated upon and carried beyond its simple origin. This happens in the final movement of Part I, 'Oh little Jesus'.

In the final chorale of Part IV, the singers and congregation sing:

> Jesus direct my beginning,
> Jesus remain ever near me,
> Jesus curb my senses,
> Jesus be my only desire,
> Jesus, remain in my thoughts always,
> Jesus, never let me falter!

Such a conclusion seems appropriate as we end the year, reminding ourselves that although Jesus was born as one of us, it is our new birth in him that brings us salvation and happiness. As we turn the page on this year, and continue our journey into the next, let us remember our own beginnings but also anticipate our own death, not with fear and loathing, but with quiet delight in the name of Jesus who turns our earthly endings into new beginnings in his kingdom!

Prayer

God and Father of our Lord Jesus Christ, he is exalted as your Son, yet humbled himself to take on human nature, being born among us and dying for us. As another year draws to a close, help us to bid farewell to the year that is past, and greet tomorrow with hope and faith renewed. Amen.

1 January

WHAT CHILD IS THIS?

In the time of King Herod, after Jesus was born in Bethlehem of Judea, wise men from the East came to Jerusalem, asking, 'Where is the child who has been born king of the Jews? For we observed his star at its rising, and have come to pay him homage.' When King Herod heard this, he was frightened, and all Jerusalem with him; and calling together all the chief priests and scribes of the people, he inquired of them where the Messiah was to be born. They told him, 'In Bethlehem of Judea; for so it has been written by the prophet: "And you, Bethlehem, in the land of Judah, are by no means least among the rulers of Judah; for from you shall come a ruler who is to shepherd my people Israel."'

MATTHEW 2:1–6

What child is this, who, laid to rest
On Mary's lap is sleeping?
Whom angels greet with anthems sweet,
While shepherds watch are keeping?
This, this is Christ the King,
Whom shepherds worship and angels sing:
Haste, haste to bring him praise,
The Babe, the son of Mary.

Why lies he in such mean estate,
Where ox and ass are feeding?
Come, have no fear, God's son is here,
His love all loves exceeding:

Nails, spear, shall pierce him through,
The cross be borne for me, for you:
Hail, hail, the Saviour comes,
The Babe, the son of Mary.

So bring him incense, gold and myrrh,
All tongues and peoples own him,
The King of kings salvation brings,
Let every heart enthrone him:
Raise, raise your song on high
While Mary sings a lullaby,
Joy, joy, for Christ is born,
The Babe, the son of Mary.

WORDS: W. CHATTERTON DIX (1837–98)
MUSIC: ENGLISH TRADITIONAL

GREENSLEEVES, the tune of this delightful carol, is one of the most famous English song tunes, and has even been attributed to King Henry VIII. Shakespeare mentions it twice in *The Merry Wives of Windsor*, and the Worshipful Company of Stationers described it as being 'new' in 1582. It may well be older than this, and was used liturgically long before the 19th century when Dix wrote the words we have here. In *The Merry Wives of Windsor*, Mistress Ford rails against Falstaff, '… but they do no more adhere and keep place together than the Hundredth Psalm to the tune of "Green Sleeves"' (Act 2, Scene 1), and this comment reveals that there may have been some attempt to use this quintessentially English tune liturgically (albeit without popular acclaim!). Later (in Act 5, Scene 5), Falstaff gets his own back on Mistress Ford and on the tune:

My doe with the black scut! Let the sky rain potatoes; let it thunder to the tune of Green Sleeves, hail kissing-comfits and snow eringoes; let there come a tempest of provocation, I will shelter me here.

During the English Civil War of the 17th century, the tune of Greensleeves was used in a song called 'The Blacksmith', or 'The Brewer', and the Cavaliers, loyal to King Charles, had various alternative texts set to it. Purely musical arrangements include a fantasia by William Byrd (1542–1623), and a more famous version by Ralph Vaughan Williams (1872–1958). GREENSLEEVES, it seems, has been much used and abused over the centuries.

The original song had at least 13 verses on the theme of unrequited love; the first verse and chorus ran thus:

> *Alas, my love, you do me wrong,*
> *To cast me off discourteously.*
> *For I have loved you well and long,*
> *Delighting in your company.*

> *Greensleeves was all my joy,*
> *Greensleeves was my delight,*
> *Greensleeves was my heart of gold,*
> *And who but my lady Greensleeves.*

The verses that follow recount the gifts that the sad lover has lavished upon the ungrateful lady, he accuses her of breaking her vows, of having spurned his loyalty and bravery, until, resigned to the loss of her love, he sings:

> *'Tis I will pray to God on high,*
> *That thou my constancy mayst see,*
> *And that yet once before I die,*
> *Thou wilt vouchsafe to love me.*

> *Ah, Greensleeves, now farewell, adieu,*
> *To God I pray to prosper thee,*
> *For I am still thy lover true,*
> *Come once again and love me.*

At this time of year, mindful of the use of 'true love' imagery in songs such as 'The Twelve Days of Christmas' and 'Tomorrow shall be my dancing day' (which we will consider from tomorrow), we can reflect on the theological and spiritual dimensions of unrequited love. Our relationship with our heavenly Father has not always been one of constancy and love; there have been rejections and denials of God throughout history. Just as the people of Israel turned away from God and spurned his love, as recounted in Isaiah and Jeremiah, we too are very capable of rejecting the loving advances made to us in the redeeming person of Christ.

The Christmas carol based on GREENSLEEVES has a specially written text by William Chatterton Dix. He was also the writer of 'As with gladness men of old', a fine Epiphany hymn. Dix was from Bristol, but spent his working life in the marine insurance business, in Glasgow, writing hymns in his spare time. 'What child is this?' was first published in Bramley and Stainer's *Christmas Carols, New and Old* in 1871. His carol retells the story of Christmas in a rather unusual question and answer form.

The question 'What child is this...?' opens the carol, and there are various answers given. Firstly, the child asleep in Mary's lap is indeed her son: 'the babe, the Son of Mary'. This fact is reiterated at the end of each verse. Whatever else we may say about this child, all appears normal and natural, a baby asleep. The gentle lilt of GREENSLEEVES, manifested in the 6/8 rhythm (two sets of three notes in a bar), musically portrays the rocking motion that parents use to get their little ones to sleep. But Dix's slightly sentimental opening, with sleeping child, angels singing and shepherds watching has a stronger line to push as we progress through the carol. Just as the original folk song 'Alas, my love' has a bittersweet flavour, so too does this carol, for in verse two we hear of the 'mean estate'—the poor location of the stable where, as sinners, we are entreated to be fearful. Be afraid, Dix warns us, be very afraid, for this silent, sleeping child, though he be the son of Mary, is the Word made flesh. The ever-so-human description of verse one is giving way to the theological meaning of this baby, of whom we may well ask, 'What child is this?'

It may not have been deliberate on Dix's part, but he has in a sense caught something of the fundamental sense of alienation that we experience when faced with a newborn infant. He or she is related to the parents, of course, but to look on a newborn is not only to encounter someone beautiful and magical and joyous, but it is also about peering into depths of strangeness and mystery. Thus, when we ask of any baby, or even of any person, 'Who is this?' we might simply be asking their name, expecting an obvious, simple answer, such as 'This is Gordon' or 'This is Maria.' At the same time there is a more profound question lurking underneath: 'Who are we, where did we come from, where are we going?' In this carol, there are elements of this ambiguity of questioning, so blithely disguised by a familiar and slightly sentimental tune.

On this eighth day after Christmas, we recall the naming and circumcision of Jesus, described in Luke 2:21: 'After eight days had passed, it was time to circumcise the child; and he was called Jesus, the name given by the angel before he was conceived in the womb.' This was a simple ceremony, but this was no ordinary little boy. We can ask questions about Jesus, sticking to the sentimental, shallow answers, or we can peer deeper, attempting to explore the significance of the Word made flesh, of Christ our king, and the way in which Mary's baby son can be both of these. While the choice is ours, here in this carol at least we can never avoid the sense that there is more than humanity being described here. And if we can grasp the dual nature of this human-divine child, asleep in Mary's arms but also awake to the sin of the world, then we too will wish to make haste to 'bring him praise' and raise his song on high!

Prayer

Christ our baby Lord, whose name is above all names, and before whom every knee shall bow, may we grow to understand the meaning of your incarnation and the power of your self-giving arrival in our fragile world. Grant us simplicity of devotion and depth of insight, so that we may never trivialize your love for us, nor lose that sense of mystery that fills and fuels our journey of faith. Amen.

THE TWELVE DAYS OF CHRISTMAS (PART I)

On the fourteenth day they rested and made that a day of feasting and gladness... Therefore the Jews of the villages, who live in the open towns, hold the fourteenth day of the month of Adar as a day for gladness and feasting, a holiday on which they send gifts of food to one another. Mordecai recorded these things, and sent letters to all the Jews who were in all the provinces of King Ahasuerus, both near and far, enjoining them that they should keep the fourteenth day of the month Adar and also the fifteenth day of the same month, year by year, as the days on which the Jews gained relief from their enemies, and as the month that had been turned for them from sorrow into gladness and from mourning into a holiday; that they should make them days of feasting and gladness, days for sending gifts of food to one another and presents to the poor.

ESTHER 9:17, 19–22

> *On the first day of Christmas my true love sent to me,*
> *a partridge in a pear tree,*
> *On the second day of Christmas my true love sent to me,*
> *two turtle doves...*
> *On the third day of Christmas my true love sent to me,*
> *three French hens...*
> *On the fourth day of Christmas my true love sent to me,*
> *four calling birds...*

On the fifth day of Christmas my true love sent to me,
five gold rings...
On the sixth day of Christmas my true love sent to me,
six geese a-laying...
On the seventh day of Christmas my true love sent to me,
seven swans a-swimming...
On the eighth day of Christmas my true love sent to me,
eight maids a-milking...
On the ninth day of Christmas my true love sent to me,
nine ladies dancing...
On the tenth day of Christmas my true love sent to me,
ten lords a-leaping...
On the eleventh day of Christmas my true love sent to me,
eleven pipers piping...
On the twelfth day of Christmas my true love sent to me,
twelve drummers drumming...

WORDS AND MUSIC: TRADITIONAL

Some people have claimed that 'The twelve days of Christmas' has its origins as a 'catechism song', learnt by both children and adults as a way of preserving a coded knowledge of the faith. It is an attractive theory, which has gained popularity in America, but Christians in Britain hardly needed to encode the basic principles of Christianity, even during the Reformation or Commonwealth periods in the 16th and 17th centuries (while there was reformation of the church, Christianity was never itself outlawed). Also, as the song is a Christmas song, its use would have been somewhat limited. On the other hand, there are other encoded songs: 'Sing a song of sixpence' is said to be about Henry VIII dissolving the monasteries, and 'Ring a ring of roses' is famously about the plague of 1665. Some com-mentators dispute this nowadays, making the radical claims that these songs are actually more or less about making pies and dancing in a circle! It always seems to be the case that where there is little fact to draw upon, speculation abounds, and whenever anyone comes up with a theory, someone else finds the means to refute it.

Therefore it is not entirely clear whether 'The twelve days of Christmas' has a history of being a deep and meaningful spiritual song or not. It seems to have its origins in France, where three versions of the song are known, and also in an English question-and-answer type of song dating from around 1625, in which each of the days is given a religious significance. This song, called 'A new dial' or 'In those twelve days', would have been sung on Twelfth Night (6 January) as part of the festivities and games that accompanied that festival. The similarities between 'A new dial' and the more famous 'The twelve days of Christmas' are striking. The 'dial' is a clock face, and the idea is to memorize tenets of faith according to the hours of the day, with the music assisting the process. While we may use 'A new dial' as a kind of key to some of the numerological symbolism that may be drawn out of 'The twelve days of Christmas', it is an interesting text in its own right, even if it is hardly ever sung today (the tune is not very inspiring). It also contains some rather unusual symbolism, which is not so obvious to us today (see 'A new dial' tomorrow).

When 'The twelve days of Christmas' was first published, in *Mirth without Mischief* in 1780, it was presented as a singing game in which anyone who forgot a verse had to pay some kind of forfeit, such as kissing someone or performing some absurd action. The spirit of such parlour games is still very much with us, although Christmas afternoon television viewing may well have replaced these traditional festive games in most households. That 'A new dial' and 'The twelve days of Christmas' were part of games with seasonally appropriate religious themes may say more about the prevailing Christian culture of the time than it does about any desire to teach the tenets of the faith. Similarly today, the game of 'charades' tells us more about our relationship with the media than it does about the actual content of any of the plays, television programmes, films or musicals illustrated in the game.

On the first day of Christmas, the true love sends a partridge in a pear tree. A tree in Christian symbolism has an obvious parallel in the tree of the cross: 'Christ redeemed us from the curse of the law by becoming a curse for us—for it is written, "Cursed is everyone who hangs on a tree"' (Galatians 3:13). The partridge gives us a clue to the French origin of the song, since partridges were first introduced into England from France in the late 1770s. Partridges, apparently, feign injury to protect their chicks. This might suggest that God, whom we take to be the true love, sent his Son Jesus on the first day of Christmas. We might also remember Jesus quoting 2 Esdras 1:30, in Luke 13:34: 'I gathered you as a hen gathers her chicks under her wings.' In art, the partridge has traditionally symbolized the church as the preserver of truth, although, unhelpfully, the partridge is compared to a thief in Jeremiah 17:11: 'Like the partridge hatching what it did not lay, so are all who amass wealth unjustly; in mid-life it will leave them, and at their end they will prove to be fools.' These are perhaps poignant words when we remember that we are discussing what many consider to be a foolish song, in which the recipient no doubt amasses a considerable amount of goods sent by the 'true love'!

On the second day, we receive two turtle doves. It is a dove that settles on Jesus at his baptism (Mark 1:10). The presence of two doves reminds us of Jesus' presentation in the temple, where Mary and Joseph 'offered a sacrifice according to what is stated in the law of the Lord, "a pair of turtle doves or two young pigeons"' (Luke 2:24; see also Leviticus 1:14; 5:7; 12:6–8). The doves themselves might represent the two Testaments, Old and New, which together make up the Bible.

The third day brings us three French hens, which were expensive birds, especially in England. These might represent the three gifts of gold, frankincense and myrrh brought by the magi to Jesus (Matthew 2:10–11). Three is a significant theological number, and so there are obvious overtones of the Trinity here. Jesus spent three days in the tomb. Another set of three might be the three virtues— faith, hope and love—as presented by Paul in 1 Corinthians 13:13. The ancient Greek mathematician Pythagorus called three the 'number of completion', because the beginning, the middle and the end make up three parts.

The 'four calling birds' of the fourth day of Christmas appears to be a corruption of 'four colly birds'. A colly bird is a blackbird, which presents us with a difficulty, as there is a legend about St Benedict in which he is supposed to have been challenged by the devil in the form of a blackbird. Benedict recognized Satan and defeated him with the sign of the cross. It is perhaps better to remember that there are four Gospels, and think of each as calling out to us across time and space with the good news of Christ incarnate.

The five gold rings are not rings at all, but ringed pheasants. These birds appear in Fra Angelico's depiction of the nativity, painted around 1440. (We can now see, incidentally, that the first seven days of the song involve birds, while the last days involve people.) There are five books in the Pentateuch—the Mosaic law—and this verse may help us to remember that. There were also five wounds of Christ, which are often marked out on the paschal candle on Easter Eve: hands, feet and side were all pierced during the crucifixion.

Just as the music of 'The twelve days of Christmas' pauses on five gold rings, so we pause, completing this first part of our numerological foray into Christmas musical games.

Prayer

God our Father, who sent your true love Jesus Christ to be our light and salvation, fill us with the delight of serving you and of making your ways known upon earth. As we relish the joys of companionship, and admire the world in which you have placed us, help us always to remember that you are the creator and ruler of all things in heaven and earth. Amen.

A NEW DIAL (THE TWELVE DAYS OF CHRISTMAS, PART 2)

1) I believe in God, the Father almighty, creator of heaven and earth. 2) I believe in Jesus Christ, his only Son, our Lord. 3) He was conceived by the power of the Holy Spirit and born of the virgin Mary. 4) He suffered under Pontius Pilate, was crucified, died, and was buried. He descended into hell [the grave]. 5) On the third day he rose again. He ascended into heaven, and is seated at the right hand of the Father. 6) He will come again to judge the living and the dead. 7) I believe in the Holy Spirit, 8) the holy catholic Church, 9) the communion of saints, 10) the forgiveness of sins, 11) the resurrection of the body, 12) and the life everlasting. Amen.

THE APOSTLES' CREED

In those twelve days let us be glad, in those twelve days let us be glad,
For God of his power hath all things made.

What are they but are but one?
One God, one baptism, and one faith, one truth there is,
the scripture saith:

What are they but are but two?
Two testaments, the old and new, we do acknowledge to be true:

What are they but are but three?
Three persons in Trinity which make one God in unity:

What are they but are but four?
Four sweet evangelists there are, Christ's birth, life, death,
which do declare:

What are they but are but five?
Five senses, like five Kings, maintain in every man a several reign:

What are they but are but six?
Six days to labour is not wrong, for God himself did work so long:

What are they but are but seven?
Seven Liberal Arts hath God sent down with divine skill
man's soul to crown:

What are they but are but eight?
Eight beatitudes are there given: use them aright and go to heaven:

What are they but are but nine?
Nine muses like the heavens' nine spheres, with sacred tunes
entice our ears:

What are they but are but ten?
Ten statutes God to Moses gave, which, kept or broke, do spill or save:

What are they but are but eleven?
Eleven thousand virgins did partake, and suffered death for Jesus' sake:

What are they but are but twelve?
Twelve are attending our God's Son: twelve make our Creed.
The dial's done.

WORDS: COLLECTED BY DAVIES GILBERT, 1822
MUSIC: TRADITIONAL

Yesterday we began to look at 'The twelve days of Christmas', and today we continue, remembering that with 'A new dial' we have two memory songs that can aid and abet our learning of basic Christian faith.

Picking up with the six geese laying eggs, these may represent the six days of creation, after which, on the seventh day, God rested (Genesis 1:24–31). Eggs are often more associated with Easter, however, where they are symbols of hope and resurrection, the chick breaking forth from the shell just as Christ breaks forth in a new dawn of salvation. In religious art, the goose is often associated with St Martin of Tours, for legend has it that it was a goose that gave away his hiding place to those who wanted to appoint him bishop of that city in the fourth century. Even today, geese are used to guard property and to make a noise if anyone approaches, so we might associate them with spiritual vigilance as recommended in 1 Peter 5:8–9: 'Discipline yourselves; keep alert. Like a roaring lion your adversary the devil prowls around, looking for someone to devour. Resist him, steadfast in your faith.'

The swan does not appear to have any particular religious significance, although in England they are all the property of the Crown. Swans are associated in ancient Greek legends with the idea of a final 'swansong', a cry that suggests they know that they are about to die. Thus they are sometimes associated with the gift of prophecy. There was also a belief that they could teach us the mysteries of music and poetry. The number seven may indicate the seven gifts of the Spirit from Romans 12:6–8: prophecy, ministry, teaching, exhortation, giving, leading and compassion. The ancient hymn *Veni creator spiritus* refers to 'thy sevenfold gifts', and there are many sevens in the book of Revelation. Seven is the number of perfection, a divine number. There are seven sacraments (eucharist, baptism, confirmation, ordination, unction, penance and marriage), and seven deadly sins: greed, avarice, envy, gluttony, lust, sloth and anger. 'A new dial' gives us a completely different use of seven: the seven 'liberal arts' of medieval education which are grammar, rhetoric, dialectic, arithmetic, geometry, astronomy and music.

As we reach the eighth day, we abandon the birdcage for persons of diverse social standing, beginning with eight milkmaids. In 'A new dial', these gentle women represent the beatitudes, found in Matthew 5:3–11, although there appear to be nine beatitudes, which confuses the issue! Eight is often associated with the resurrection, as Christ rose on the eighth day. This is why some baptismal fonts are octagonal. The significance of milkmaids is not clear, although we might be reminded of the apostle Paul's words: 'I fed you with milk, not solid food, for you were not ready for solid food' (1 Corinthians 3:2). Just as milk is the basic source of food and life, provided at the mother's breast, so is the gospel the nourishment of our souls.

If we follow 'A new dial', nine is the number of the 'muses' or goddesses of classical Greek education: astronomy, music, epic poetry, history, love poetry, comedy, sacred poetry, dancing and tragedy. Nine can also refer to the fruit of the Spirit described in Galatians 5:22–23. These are love, joy, peace, patience, kindness, generosity, faithfulness, gentleness and self-control. That the nine ladies dance might remind us of Miriam dancing in Exodus 15:20–21. Spiritual dancing, although it has recently become more popular, has for centuries been viewed with some suspicion. In Exodus 32:19 it is dancing that makes Moses destroy the tablets of the Ten Commandments, and in Judges 11:34 we hear of Jepthah's unfortunate daughter dancing out to meet him.

Individual cases aside, dancing is an expression of joy and delight and, appropriately directed, such dancing can be a celebration of the abundant gift of life that Christ brings us (John 10:10). Today we might also be reminded of Sydney Carter's famous hymn 'Lord of the dance', which describes the life, death and resurrection of Christ as a kind of eternal dance, which 'still goes on' (also see 'Tomorrow shall be my dancing day', 4 January, p. 189).

The ten leaping lords remind us of the Ten Commandments. 'I am the Lord your God, who brought you out of the land of Egypt, out of the house of slavery,' says the first commandment; 'you shall have no other gods before me' (Exodus 20:2–3). Jesus sometimes criticized the Jewish leaders because they behaved as though the law were their God, as though they had ten 'Lords', almost. The Ten

Commandments are the basis of the Jewish faith, and therefore are also paramount in Christianity (Jesus never denounced them, but rather sought to uphold them). In John 13:34 (also 15:12) Jesus gives us a new, eleventh commandment: '… that you love one another. Just as I have loved you, you also should love one another'.

Eleven pipers are taken to represent the eleven named disciples who remained faithful to Christ after the betrayal by Judas. Later, Matthias was appointed by the casting of lots (Acts 1:22–26). There is actually very little reference to music or musicians in the New Testament, although nowadays music holds a privileged and special place in Christian worship. We seldom hear pipes, other than those of the organ used in worship, but Jesus' enigmatic phrase, 'We played the flute for you, and you did not dance' does spring to mind (Luke 7:32).

Finally, there are a dozen drummers banging away. We might want to associate twelve with the apostles (but see 'eleven'), or with the twelve tribes of Israel: Reuben, Simeon, Levi, Judah, Issachar, Zebulun, Benjamin, Dan, Naphtali, Gad, Asher and Joseph. 'A new dial' prefers twelve as defining sections of the Apostles' Creed. These twelve statements articulate Christian belief: they are the drumbeat of faith.

Today, 'The twelve days of Christmas' can be useful precisely for the purpose that many doubt it originally had. These humorous, memorable lines still lend themselves as a teaching aid in an age that may have forgotten some of the basics of faith, if it ever knew them. At Christmas-time, when many people make a rare appearance in church, there may well be a place for this rather odd Christmas nursery rhyme.

The key, of course, lies in its numerological structure. Each numbered day has a resonance with something numerical in our faith, and it is not hard to remember, discover or even invent a connection. The numbers one to twelve can all remind us of Christian truths, as we have seen. That other Christmas song, 'A new dial', helps us here, for it more explicitly uses music, numerology and theology to enliven and elucidate the faith revealed in Jesus Christ and handed down through the ages in such creative, even strange, ways.

Prayer

O Lord, to whom all shall give account, number us among your chosen people, fill us with the vision of eternity, and grant that we may turn to you each hour of every day, ever inspired by the range and depth of your love revealed in creation and in the saving work of Jesus Christ, your Son, our Lord. Amen.

4 January

TOMORROW SHALL BE MY DANCING DAY

For everything there is a season, and a time for every matter under heaven: a time to be born, and a time to die; a time to plant, and a time to pluck up what is planted; a time to kill, and a time to heal; a time to break down, and a time to build up; a time to weep, and a time to laugh; a time to mourn, and a time to dance; a time to throw away stones, and a time to gather stones together; a time to embrace, and a time to refrain from embracing; a time to seek, and a time to lose; a time to keep, and a time to throw away; a time to tear, and a time to sew; a time to keep silence, and a time to speak; a time to love, and a time to hate; a time for war, and a time for peace... He has made everything suitable for its time; moreover, he has put a sense of past and future into their minds, yet they cannot find out what God has done from the beginning to the end.

ECCLESIASTES 3:1–8, 11

> *Tomorrow shall be my dancing day:*
> *I would my true love did so chance*
> *To see the legend of my play,*
> *To call my true love to my dance:*
> *Sing, O my love,*
> *This have I done for my true love.*

In a manger laid and wrapped I was,
So very poor this was my chance,
Betwixt an ox and a silly poor ass,
To call my true love to my dance:

Then was I born of a virgin pure,
Of her I took fleshly substance;
Thus was I knit to man's nature,
To call my true love to my dance:

Then afterwards baptized I was;
The Holy Ghost on me did glance,
My Father's voice heard from above,
To call my true love to my dance:

WORDS AND MUSIC: TRADITIONAL
ALSO MUSIC: JOHN GARDNER (B. 1917)

As I hinted yesterday, dance has had a chequered spiritual history, during which it has often been alienated, proscribed or at best ignored. The Prayer Book of 1559 drawn up by Archbishop Thomas Cranmer had a motif of the 'Dance of Death' as an illustration alongside the psalms, and the artist Hans Holbein created a series of woodcut drawings in 1538 which include 'The alphabet of Death', in which each letter has a morbid theme. In another picture, 'The new-married lady', the character of Death insidiously dances before the bride and groom, beating a tambour. Old St Paul's Cathedral, destroyed in the great London fire of 1666, had similarly macabre carvings lining the cloisters, illustrating sinister verses written by the poet John Lydgate, who was a contemporary of Chaucer.

More recently, the French composer Camille Saint-Saëns (1835–1921) wrote his famous *Danse Macabre* in which the plain-song tune to the *Dies Irae* (part of the Latin funeral service) forms the musical theme, with xylophones illustrating rattling bones while 'Death' retunes his violin, creating a weird and wonderful clash representing the discord between the worlds of the living and the dead.

But it is not all bad news for Christian devotees of dance, for in opposition to the Dance of Death, we might consider the 'Dance of Life', which also has a long history. Many people are familiar with the hymn 'Lord of the dance', written in 1963. by Sidney Carter (who died in 2004) The hymn's origins in folk music are clear: the tune that Carter used comes from the American Appalachian mountain region (it was originally known as ''Tis a gift to be simple'), which the composer Aaron Copland also used in his orchestral work *Appalachian Spring,* completed in 1944. What is perhaps not so well known is the tradition from which Carter's hymn wells up. 'Lord of the dance' owes a great deal of homage to a much older carol called 'Tomorrow shall be my dancing day', which also characterizes the story of Christ's life as a kind of dance.

The text of 'Tomorrow shall be my dancing day' was first published in 1833, but almost certainly has its origin in the medieval mystery plays, which often ended with a processional dance. The actor playing Christ would sing the verses, and actors and audience would dance and sing during the refrain. It was also not unusual for the character of the baby Jesus to sing a song foretelling his life, mission and purpose. Thus the carol actually has twelve verses in total, although the four reproduced here are the ones most often heard today. Other verses tell of the temptations in the wilderness, the betrayal by Judas, the trials and scourging by Pilate, the crucifixion and piercing, the descent to hell and the resurrection and ascension. As a result, there is a sense in which this carol could be used throughout the year, although it has been saddled with a Christmas flavour and is therefore neglected. It does make a good carol for Epiphanytide, however, and better still for the feast of the baptism of Christ, which is usually celebrated on the Sunday after Epiphany. It is perhaps a little strange that we move so quickly from the visit of the magi to the baptism of Christ, but this carol reminds us that in scripture the account of the baptism of Christ does more or less follow that of the birth narratives (Luke inserts the story of Jesus with the teachers in the temple, Luke 2:41–52). During the season of Epiphanytide, between 6 January and 2 February (Candlemas), it is good to reflect on those three 'revealings' of Christ: his encounter with the magi, his baptism, and the turning of water into wine at Cana (John 2:1–11). Bishop Christopher Wordsworth (1807–85) articulated this dimension of the Epiphany season when he wrote:

> *Manifest at Jordan's stream,*
> *Prophet, Priest, and King supreme;*
> *And at Cana wedding-guest*
> *In thy Godhead manifest;*
> *Manifest in power divine,*
> *Changing water into wine;*
> *Anthems be to thee addrest,*
> *God in Man made manifest.*

While the carol itself may have medieval origins, the idea of Christ as 'my true love' not only reminds us of 'The twelve days of Christmas' but also carries us back to the Song of Songs, the love poetry of the Old Testament, the rich and suggestive language of which has often been treated as allegorical, representing the union between Christ and the church. 'Tomorrow shall be my dancing day' is not only a love song, it is also a wedding dance, hinting at an intimacy between Christ and church that takes as its model the human experience of loving relationship.

Such a sensual carol demands a certain kind of music, and there are various versions to choose from. The tune given in the *Oxford Book of Carols* is that provided by William Sandys, who published it first in his *Christmas Carols Ancient and Modern* in 1833. That tune has a gentle swing to it that combines elements of waltz with lullaby. Since then, other composers have written more adventurous music, among them John Rutter (b. 1945), Geoffrey Burgon (b. 1941), and John Gardner (b. 1917).

Gardner is a neglected composer whose talent exceeds his fame.

Born in Manchester, he spent his youth in the West Country before studying at Oxford with Parry (the composer of 'Jerusalem'). He taught at various institutions, including Morley College and St Paul's Girls' School (where Gustav Holst had also taught), and he taught composition at the Royal Academy of Music. As well as concerti, symphonies and operas, Gardner wrote exquisite short pieces, of which 'Tomorrow shall be my dancing day' is a fine example. Rock and jazz have influenced his work, and this can be heard not only in 'Tomorrow shall be my dancing day' but also in his delightful children's opera *Bel and the Dragon*, written in 1973.

Gardner's delightful, slightly jazzy version of 'Tomorrow shall be my dancing day' has become popular in recent years, because it is such fun to sing. The organ part is surprisingly light and some performers bring in a percussionist as well, to convey not only a sense of the dance but also the exuberance of the text. The music alternates between a rhythmic introductory passage and a smoother dance theme: it is straightforward but very effective, often raising a smile from audience and chorister alike.

As the writer of Ecclesiastes tells us, there is a time for everything, and the same is true in worship. Variety has often been thought of as the 'spice of life', and in our day we have become accustomed to Christian worship taking many forms and drawing on many styles. While the relationship between dance and faith has not always been a good one, Christmas and Easter carols such as 'Lord of the dance' and 'Tomorrow shall be my dancing day' have brought the two together in a popular and acceptable way. On another plane, liturgical dance is becoming more mainstream in worship, and it would appear that the art form is at last gaining respect and value as an expression of faith.

We are also very used to Christian worship in all life circumstances, especially birth (baptism), marriage and death. Just as there is a time to be born and a time to die, so there are liturgical events to mark those crucial and inevitable moments of joy or grief. We are also reminded that there is a time for war and for peace, which might make us wonder whether it is perhaps 'right' to fight sometimes, or to speak out. Such situations are by no means only to be found in the distant past, but arise in each and every generation. We find these fundamental truths of human existence to which Ecclesiastes refers in any period of time, past or present, and yet, as he reminds us, we 'cannot find out what God has done from the beginning to the end' (3:11). Life, with all its ups and downs, dances and sorrows, is still a great mystery to us. But in its diversity and regularity is to be found something of God, our creator, our redeemer, our sustainer, who partners us in the dances of both life and death, leading us onward and upward to our heavenly rest.

Prayer

Jesus, you are Lord of the dance and victor over death. Help our souls to dance to the music of your mercy, and our hearts to beat to the rhythms of your praise, so that at any time and in every place we may be ever mindful that you are the same yesterday, today and tomorrow. Amen.

AHMAL AND THE NIGHT VISITORS

Then Jesus, filled with the power of the Spirit, returned to Galilee, and a report about him spread through all the surrounding country. He began to teach in their synagogues and was praised by everyone. When he came to Nazareth, where he had been brought up, he went to the synagogue on the sabbath day, as was his custom. He stood up to read, and the scroll of the prophet Isaiah was given to him. He unrolled the scroll and found the place where it was written: 'The Spirit of the Lord is upon me, because he has anointed me to bring good news to the poor. He has sent me to proclaim release to the captives and recovery of sight to the blind, to let the oppressed go free, to proclaim the year of the Lord's favour.' And he rolled up the scroll, gave it back to the attendant, and sat down. The eyes of all in the synagogue were fixed on him. Then he began to say to them, 'Today this scripture has been fulfilled in your hearing.' All spoke well of him and were amazed at the gracious words that came from his mouth. They said, 'Is not this Joseph's son?'

LUKE 4:14–22

In 1951, the Italian composer Gian Carlo Menotti (b. 1911) was asked by the National Broadcasting Company (NBC) to compose the first opera written especially for television, to be broadcast in the USA on Christmas Eve that year. The task was certainly a daunting one: the idea that millions of people might be watching does not trouble Olympic athletes and newsreaders today, but it is so easy for us to forget (if we are old enough!) what the early days of television were like. Even as November began, Menotti had not the first idea what to write about. The solution was to be found in a painting attributed to Hieronymous Bosch, 'The Adoration of the Magi', which he saw in the Metropolitan Museum of Art in New York. It depicts, kneeling before the Madonna and child, not only three wise men but also peasants and curious onlookers. As far as Menotti was concerned, the three kings in this painting brought him a gift—the inspiration for a successful and popular hour-long opera called *Ahmal and the Night Visitors*.

The story is that of a young boy who lives with his mother. She is very poor, and he cannot walk without a crutch. One night, the three magi visit them on their way to Bethlehem. Ahmal is astonished, and his mother does not believe him when he tells her that there is a king at the door. She knows he has a vivid imagination, and accuses him of fibbing. Twice he returns, admitting his error: there is not a king at the door, but two kings... and then three! The kings are not only bearing gifts; they also bring with them a wondrous story, a tale of the birth of a Saviour whom they intend to visit.

Ahmal's mother is awed and humbled, and she sends her son to tell the local shepherds, who soon appear offering food, for which the kings are grateful. Then the shepherds dance, accompanied by Ahmal, playing his shepherd's pipes. Menotti portrays their dancing as at first hesitant, betraying their nervousness, but becoming more confident as the music builds to a whirling tarantella. (A tarantella is an Italian dance, fast and furious, which one supposedly dances after having been bitten by a tarantula spider!)

After the excitement and dancing, everyone turns in for the night except Ahmal's mother, who lies awake, troubled by how much even one of those gifts might help her poor crippled son. Tormented into action, she steals some gold. She is caught, however, and berated by the kings. Meanwhile, Ahmal wakes up and tries to help his terrified mother by rushing to her aid, crying, 'Don't you dare hurt my mother!' King Melchior forgives her attempted theft, and says that the child they are looking for hardly needs gold anyway. Instead, he tells her, Jesus will build his kingdom on love, and the keys of his city belong to the poor. 'He will soon walk among us,' Melchior sings, and 'He will bring us new life and receive our death.'

These words touch the mother's heart, and in spite of being offered the gold she tried to take, she now rejects it, saying that she has waited so long for such a child as they describe, and she would send a gift of her own if only she could. Ahmal interjects, suggesting that they send Jesus his crutch ('who knows, he may need one,' he sings). His mother says that he can't do such a thing, but a miracle has begun. As Ahmal raises his crutch to offer it as a gift to send to Bethlehem, he realizes that he doesn't need it any more. The kings and their page are in awe of Ahmal now, and want to touch him, because he has been touched by God. Ahmal says he wants to go to Bethlehem too, so that he can give thanks to the holy child who has evidently healed him. His mother agrees, and they depart, Ahmal playing his pipes as they recede into the snowy landscape.

This delightful story, with its English text and accessible music, has found a central place in the Christmas repertoire, especially in the United States. Melody abounds in this straightforward opera, and Menotti himself said that he saw *Ahmal* as a doorway into opera for children. The same could almost be said of its theology. Set out as a kind of fairy tale (Menotti wrote the libretto too), it may seem lightweight theologically, and we might even be wary of the artistic licence taken with the figures of the three kings (Matthew 2:1–12 does not specify kings, or that there were three of them). On the other hand, Menotti's treatment of these three characters, one of whom is portrayed as being rather deaf and a bit crazy, humanizes these magi from the mists of Matthew's Gospel, and children may well come to learn more of the real story that lies behind this folk-like tale. Nor is the story lacking in spiritual depth: its overall message speaks of good news for the poor and lame, forgiveness for transgressors, and of how charity and selfless love can lead to miracles, which in turn lead to praise and thanksgiving.

Although the work was a very successful experiment in television opera, Menotti was cautious about that medium, which the world now takes for granted. Writing a programme note for a 1963 production, he wrote about those who watch television casually:

The spectator who takes no journey and has no appointed time or seat, but, carelessly clad, sits casually on the first available chair in his living room, and who, knitting or perhaps playing with the kitten, 'turns on' what he takes to be a theatrical performance, will never know the emotion of a real theatrical experience... (the artist) addresses you in utter dignity—whether his message be comic or tragic—and to partake in his experience, you must share this seriousness and receive his message wearing your 'Sunday clothes'.

The same might be said for worship. Menotti's words remind us that while we can project and receive our experiences of anything through almost any medium, there is a lot to be said for really partaking—for getting involved, being there, rather than simply being observers, judges or spectators. Ahmal realizes this when he desires to go and thank the Christ-child himself. We watch Ahmal's mother struggle with her poverty, and we watch Ahmal offer his crutch to Jesus, and we are moved—we feel involved. Worship, like art, is a two-way engagement. It is not a show, like something on television, which we can dip into, or play with at Christmas-time when all the nice carols get sung. Worship, like art, requires a bit of effort, and is not a spectator's exercise in observation. It is about relationship, with God and with those who also partake.

In *Ahmal*, King Kaspar has a box in which he keeps all kinds of beads, sweets and playthings, and he never travels without it. Most of us have a box plugged in at home, which we wouldn't do without. For some, the television truly is a substitute for companionship, a window on the world, a source of pleasure and information. This Christmas, though, let's leave home, like Ahmal, throwing away the televisual prop, and let us head to Bethlehem to give real thanks and praise to the Christ-child, before whom shepherds and kings adored and angels sang!

More importantly, let us remind ourselves of the message of good news and release proclaimed by Christ. In the passage from Luke, we see him, Spirit-filled, proclaiming that the promise articulated by Isaiah is fulfilled in their hearing. It must have been a spine-tingling moment as Jesus read the ancient document, indicating that he was the saving one to whom it refers. This manifesto of grace that he read was handed on to his generation through the Jewish tradition, and it has been transmitted to us by the first apostles and Gospel writers, who began broadcasting the good news two thousand years ago. While there has been much interference, and some places where the gospel is yet to be heard, the signal is still loud and clear. In Jesus, the Son of God, there is hope for all people, release from poverty, imprisonment and blindness. This God has done by sending Jesus, the incarnate bearer of truth and love, through whom we have direct access to the Father (Ephesians 2:18; 3:12).

Prayer

O Lord Jesus Christ, you are the medium and the message of our salvation. We give you thanks and praise for the glorious mystery of your birth and the miracle of your incarnation. Inspire and assist us always to care for the poor and needy, and let us never lean on anything other than the hope and joy you bring us. Amen.

WE THREE KINGS

Herod secretly called for the wise men and learned from them the exact time when the star had appeared. Then he sent them to Bethlehem, saying, 'Go and search diligently for the child; and when you have found him, bring me word so that I may also go and pay him homage.' When they had heard the king, they set out; and there, ahead of them, went the star that they had seen at its rising, until it stopped over the place where the child was. When they saw that the star had stopped, they were overwhelmed with joy. On entering the house, they saw the child with Mary his mother; and they knelt down and paid him homage. Then, opening their treasure-chests, they offered him gifts of gold, frankincense, and myrrh.

MATTHEW 2:7–11

We three kings of Orient are;
Bearing gifts we traverse afar
Field and fountain, moor and mountain,
Following yonder star:

O star of wonder, star of night,
Star with royal beauty bright,
Westward leading, still proceeding,
Guide us to thy perfect light.

Born a king on Bethlehem plain,
Gold I bring, to crown him again—
King for ever, ceasing never,
Over us all to reign:

Frankincense to offer have I;
Incense owns a deity nigh:
Prayer and praising, all men raising,
Worship him, God most high:

Myrrh is mine; its bitter perfume
Breathes a life of gathering gloom;
Sorrowing, sighing, bleeding, dying,
Sealed in the stone-cold tomb:

Glorious now, behold him arise,
King, and God, and sacrifice!
Heav'n sings alleluya,
Alleluya the earth replies:

WORDS AND MUSIC: J.H. HOPKINS (1820–91)

'We three kings of orient are' is probably the best-known of all Epiphany carols. It is also the one that is most often brought forward into the Christmas season for use at carol services and in nativity plays. This is because it is so easy to learn and sing, and even very young children can manage the refrain. Furthermore, what we have here is a straightforward dramatization of the story of the wise men's visit to Jesus, as recounted in Matthew 2:1–11.

The carol was first published in 1884, and its author, the Revd Dr John Hopkins, was Rector of Williamsport in Pennsylvania. He wrote it as part of a Christmas pageant for the General Theological Seminary in New York City. Hopkins, composer of many carols and hymns, wrote both the words and the music, which is somewhat unusual. This does mean, however, that there are certain issues about this carol which we can lay squarely at his door! For example, the refrain begins 'O... star of wonder...', and while Hopkins was quite explicit that there should be no slowing down or dragging of the word 'O', there is such a diversity of interpretation over the potential slowing up before each refrain, that the musicians leading have to give a very strong lead indeed—once they have made their own mind up, of course!

Any criticism of Hopkins' music must then give way to a recognition of his misleading text, the consequences of which have to be addressed every Christmas all over the English-speaking world. The simple fact is that those people who visited Christ from eastern lands were not kings; nor were there three of them. Yet so many children, nurtured on this carol, carry into adult life this misconception so carelessly promulgated by the Revd Dr Hopkins. As a parish clergyman, he should have known better...

Of course, he did know better, and if we look into the carol a bit more deeply, we discover that his use of 'three kings' is quite deliberate and points us towards traditions other than the strictly biblical one. Origen (c.185–c.254) first suggested that there were three gift-bearers, largely because three gifts are mentioned and it was assumed from an early date that they brought one each. The tradition that they might have been kings is more complicated. A sixth-century tradition gives the 'kings' the names of Caspar, Balthasar and Melchior. These names are often used when 'We three kings' is sung, and sometimes soloists take their roles. In some churches the drama is heightened further, with the carol being sung in procession around the building: as each 'king' sings their verse, the related gift of gold, frankincense or myrrh is presented at the crib or altar.

The origin of the kings' names comes from an ancient custom of blessing homes at the beginning of each year on the feast of the Epiphany. As with any Christian holy day, the observation of the feast may begin on the previous evening. According to a tradition that predates the Middle Ages, the Latin blessing *Christus mansionem benedicat* ('May Christ bless this home') would be said, while the first letters of the words were inscribed above the doorway of the house. The chalk used for writing these letters, C-M-B, would have been previously blessed, and it is from this practice that we still find in some schools a tradition of blessing the chalk to be used during the year. Of course, in this age of whiteboards and marker pens, some of the historical significance is lost!

The names Caspar, Melchior and Balthasar were invented as an *aide-memoire* for the blessing, and became inextricably associated with it. Thus in Germany, dried herbs would be burnt and their aroma would fill the house. Doorways would be sprinkled with holy water and the master of the house would write 'CMB' and the year in chalk above the house and barn door, saying, *'Caspar, Melchior, Balthasar, behütet uns auch für dieses Jahr, vor Feuer und vor Wassergefahr'* ('Caspar, Melchior, Balthasar, protect us again this year from the dangers of fire and water').

Built into this ancient tradition is the idea of a new start and a new year. We begin our new year on 1 January, of course, but New Year's Day falls in the midst of the Christmas season, and is itself known as the feast of the naming of Jesus. In societies and ages that were much more ecclesiastically minded than ours is now, it made far more sense to consider the feast of the Epiphany to be the end of one season and the beginning of another. In the West, Christmas was 25 December and Epiphany (the 'revealing' of Christ) was 6 January, twelve days later. This is why we speak of 'twelve days of Christmas'. Only when the twelve days are over is there really a sense of moving away from Christmas towards the recently welcomed new year. It is almost as if, on the last day of Christmas, the wise men not only bring gifts but they also herald the new year ahead. Christmas is over, and so we push on towards Candlemas and thence to Lent (Candlemas is 40 days after Christmas, on 2 February, and marks the celebration of Christ's presentation in the temple as recounted in Luke 2:22–38). In 2005, Ash Wednesday fell only a week after Candlemas.

So it is appropriate that we end our Christmas season here, saying farewell as the wise men greet Jesus. Their arrival fulfils the psalmist's prophecy: 'May the kings of Tarshish and of the isles render him tribute, may the kings of Sheba and Seba bring gifts. May all kings fall down before him, all nations give him service... Long may he live! May gold of Sheba be given to him' (Psalm 72:10–11, 15).

With Christmas now over, we can take down our Christmas trees and decorations, plunder the tree for goodies and look forward to the new term and the lengthening of the days. As with much of Christmas, there is a blend of the holy with the pagan, the religious with the secular, the special with the mundane. Throughout this period we have seen how traditions have been created out of pagan or Christian beliefs and practices, but they have interacted with each other, sometimes leading to the Christianization of a pagan practice, as with the feast of Christmas itself, or vice versa. Some of the ingredients of Christmas have changed from being pagan to being Christian, but others have become almost pagan as people have forgotten their heritage.

We might be pleased that the holly and the ivy have acquired Christian symbolism (they were originally pagan fertility symbols representing male and female, but now represent resurrection and eternal life respectively), and yet lament misguided attempts to remove Jesus from Christmas. So let us end as we began. Let us be vigilant and watchful, waiting for our Lord and ensuring that Christmas never becomes less than what it truly is: the celebration of Christ's nativity, the welcoming, each year, of God made flesh, revealed among us, now and until the end of time.

Prayer

O King of kings and Lord of lords, who was born at Bethlehem and revealed to the nations as God among us, grant us a portion of your heavenly wisdom, that we may always be guided on our journey by the light of your salvation, shining for all the world to see. Amen.

SUGGESTIONS FOR GROUP DISCUSSION OR INDIVIDUAL REFLECTION

It is very common in churches these days to have Lent study courses, but Advent courses are probably less common. Nevertheless, the opportunities for fellowship, reflection and 'time out' can be particularly valuable in the hectic pre-Christmas period. It is perhaps a very noble and fortunate group that is able to meet between Christmas and New Year, or between New Year and Epiphany, but an opportunity to reflect together at that time can help to ground us in the true meaning of the festivities.

In an attempt to be both realistic and encouraging in this respect, here are some topics and questions that might be used as the basis for a group meeting, or for personal reflection. Where groups use this material, it will be beneficial to add opening and closing prayers (offered at the end of each chapter), time for recapitulation of the previous week's issues and opportunity for sharing ideas and experiences.

Where hymns are suggested, I have given the numbers as found in *Common Praise*, Canterbury Press, 2000 (CP), and *Complete Anglican Hymns Old and New*, Kevin Mayhew, 2000 (HON). The words are to be found in this book, of course! Recordings can be purchased on the Internet, or even downloaded from some websites, or borrowed from local libraries. The ubiquitous amazon.co.uk is always a good place to start. Wherever possible, I have given the complete reference code for a CD, but in most cases there is more than one recording available, and it is not necessary to use the one I have recommended. The usual format for describing a CD is composer (where appropriate), title, artist(s), conductor, record label, code number, year of release.

First week of Advent: Procession into Advent

Listen to a recording of the Advent Responsory (*Advent at St Paul's*, St Paul's Cathedral Choir, Scott, Hyperion, CDA66994, 1997) and/or 'Come, thou redeemer of the earth'—or sing the latter (CP49) (*Advent and Christmas at Portsmouth Cathedral*, Portsmouth Cathedral Choir, Froggatt, York Ambisonics, YORKCD835, 2002). Read Isaiah 9:1–6

1. Have you ever been to an Advent carol service? Describe what happened. What significance or relevance does the 'procession of Advent' have today?
2. What is your impression of the ancient texts of Advent that are still in use today? To what extent do we only know them today because they have been preserved in musical works?
3. What do you think about the way hymn writers take scripture and adapt it poetically? Should we regard an ancient hymn as equal to scripture, or merely as a commentary upon it?
4. Think about your expectations and hopes for the coming month. In what way will you be or feel any different by the time we reach Christmas?
5. What is the point of Advent?

Sing or listen to 'Lo! He comes with clouds descending' (CP31; HON405).

Second week of Advent: Father Christmas

Begin by singing or listening to 'Thou whose almighty word' (CP267; HON684).
Read 1 Timothy 3.

1. What do you know about St Nicholas? Do you approve of the way in which he has mutated into Father Christmas?
2. Should children be told that Father Christmas does (not) exist? Why? How can St Nicholas help us with the mission and ministry of the church in this day and age?
3. If you can, listen to some (or all) of Britten's Cantata (Britten, *St Nicholas*, ECO and Corydon Singers, Best, Hyperion, 66333, 1988). How is this like the Father Christmas we know and love?
4. What do you want for Christmas? How do you react to being made to wait for things? (Can you wait for anything or are you like a child on Christmas Eve who cannot sleep for anticipation?)
5. What are we really waiting for? What do you really believe is going to happen?

Finish by prayerfully singing (or listening to) the Taizé chant 'Wait for the Lord' (*My Soul is at Rest—Songs of Taizé* Volume 2, Kingsway, KMCD 841, 1995).

Third week of Advent: John and Justice

Begin by singing 'Born in the night' (HON80).
Read John 1:6–39.

1. Have a look at some of Raphael's paintings of Jesus with John the Baptist. How do they strike you?

   (See www.abcgallery.com/R/raphael/raphael.html)

   Reflect for a little while on the relationship between John and Jesus throughout their young lives. In what sense is it right to think of John as a Christian martyr (someone who dies witnessing to the resurrection of Christ)?
2. Listen to Gibbons' 'This is the record of John' (*Advent at St Paul's*, St Paul's Cathedral Choir, Scott, Hyperion, 66994, 1997). What impact does the use of a high male alto voice have? How would John have come across to the people of his day? How does he come across now? (You may like to look at the chapter on Richard Strauss' opera *Salome* in *The Harmony of Heaven*, BRF 2003, pp. 138–141, or the chapter 'On Jordan's Bank' in *The Music of Praise*, BRF 2002, pp. 54–57).
3. Identify some situations today where issues of justice for the poor and needy are still of concern. Reflect on the response of aid from peoples and governments, such as in December 2004 when the tsunami struck south-east Asia. How do John's ascetic lifestyle and Jesus' humble birth speak to these situations? How can we admire glorious paintings and wonderful music when others suffer and perish through natural or humanly created violence or disaster?
4. Is it realistic to suppose that Christ might walk in our streets again—or how might he already be doing so?

Finish by listening to John Tavener's anthem 'The Lamb' (Tavener, *Christmas Proclamation*, St John's College, Cambridge, Robinson, Naxos, 8555256, 2002).

Fourth week of Advent: O Come, Emmanuel

Begin by singing or listening to 'O come, O come, Emmanuel' (CP32; HON480).

1. Consider the Advent antiphons on which the verses are based. What do they mean? Consider what they meant when they were written, and what they might mean for us today. Can you think of situations to which these antiphons speak? For whom might they be helpful? What is going on here—what are we calling on Christ to be for us, both here and now and upon his return?
2. Listen to some or all of James MacMillan's piece 'Veni, veni, Emmanuel' (MacMillan, *Veni, veni, Emmanuel*, Scottish Chamber Orchestra, Glennie, BMG 09026–61916, 1993). How does this piece strike you? Do you like it?
3. Christmas is approaching fast, and has been evident in the shops for many weeks. Is our sense of anticipation coming to an end? How can we prevent Christmas from being an anticlimax?
4. Listen to a setting of 'Adam lay ybounden' (*Carols from Kings*, King's College, Cambridge, Willcocks & Ledger, EMI Classics, CDCAROL1, 1997). What do you make of the text?
5. Read Genesis 3. Is it right to say that it was a good thing that Adam sinned because it enabled the incarnation, passion and resurrection of Christ? Wouldn't it have been better if Adam and Eve had behaved themselves?
6. What would life be like if they had? What will it be like after Jesus returns? How would you explain Adam's sin and Christ's return to a non-Christian?

Finish by singing 'Of the father's heart begotten' (CP65; HON486).

Christmas week or New Year's week: Religion at Christmas

Sing or listen to 'Masters in this hall' (*Songs of Angels—Christmas Hymns and Carols*, Shaw Chamber Singers, Shaw, Telarc, CD80377, 1994).

1. This whole period is part of the Christmas season, liturgically speaking. How pagan has your Christmas been? How can the traditions of light, mistletoe and pudding, indulgence and television be reconciled with the original and true meaning of the incarnation?
2. Reflect on the Christmas cards you have sent or received (group members may like to bring along examples). What are the pictures saying? What are the greetings inside saying about the people who have sent them and the spirit in which they are sent? What can we learn from our Christmas cards about the friends and acquaintances who send them, and also about society as a whole? What do you really feel about the sending of Christmas cards: is it a good thing, a bad thing, or an inevitable chore?

Read Luke 1:26–56. Listen to a setting of the *Ave Maria* (*Ave Maria—Sacred Arias and Choruses*, Hungarian Radio Chorus, Antal et al, Naxos, 8553751, 1997).

3. Does the *Ave Maria* appeal or does it annoy you? Reflect and pray about your response to it. What do you feel about religious conflict? Where are there religious conflicts happening around us now, and why? How can or should such conflict be avoided? What does the Magnificat have to contribute to this debate?

Finish by singing a popular Christmas carol, such as 'Hark! the herald angels sing' (CP53; HON266) or 'Once in royal David's city' (CP66; HON521).

Epiphany Week: Twelfth Night and Tomorrow

Listen to or sing 'The twelve days of Christmas' (*Our Christmas Songs for You*, London Voices, te Kanawa et al, EMI Classics, CDC5561762, 1996).
Say the Apostles' Creed together.

1. What do you think about the idea that this song might have religious significance? Whether it was intended to or not, do you find numerological interpretations of it helpful, or are you happier with it as a simple folk-tune nonsense game?
2. If you want a bit of fun, try to rewrite the song, beginning with 'On the first day of Christmas, Jesus gave to me...'
3. Think about the power of music to influence opinion and change lives. Consider some contemporary writers: what contribution have Graham Kendrick, Taizé and Iona made to our worshipping life?
4. How important is music in your life? Is Jesus your true love? Are the two connected in any way?
5. Read Matthew 2:1–11. Would you make such a journey? Is there an equivalent today? How is the debate about whether the magi were wise men, kings or astrologers relevant today? What is the true meaning of Epiphany and why does it mark the beginning of a season that lasts nearly a month?
6. What will next Christmas be like? How do you think the world will have changed? How will you have changed?

Finish by listening to 'Tomorrow shall be my dancing day', preferably John Gardiner's setting (*Carols from Christ Church*, Christ Church Cathedral Choir, Grier, ASV White Line, CDWHL2097, 1996).

THE HARMONY OF HEAVEN

Musical meditations for Lent and Easter

Lent is a time for prayer, for Bible study and also for music. Some of the greatest music ever written was written for worship during Lent and Easter, but all kinds of other music can also resonate for us at this time in the Church's year, touching on questions of truth, beauty, love, right and wrong, despair and hope, death and life.

This book brings together a daily Bible reading and comment for every day from Ash Wednesday to Easter Monday together with reflection on a wealth of music that has some special relevance to the themes of this season, from Handel's *Messiah* and Bach's *St John Passion* to *Carnival of the Animals* and *Peter and the Wolf!*

ISBN 1 84101 334 X   £7.99
Available from your local Christian bookshop or, in case of difficulty, direct from BRF using the order form on page 221.

THE MUSIC OF PRAISE

Through the Church year with the great hymns

This is a book of 52 meditations on well-known hymns from 'Amazing Grace' to 'When I Survey the Wondrous Cross', exploring the meaning and message of the words, the beauty of the music, and their continuing relevance and inspiration for people today. It is also a journey through the Christian year with the hymn writers and musicians who have promoted and sustained the faith of millions, yesterday and today.

Each meditation is accompanied by the full text of the hymn, plus a concluding prayer, which can be used for private reflection or public worship.

ISBN 1 84101 237 8   £12.99
Available from your local Christian bookshop or, in case of difficulty, direct from BRF using the order form on page 221.

THE ART OF WAITING

Daily reflections for the Advent season

Wendy Bray

'Almost every part of our daily lives involves a mix of waiting, planning and anticipation. From the simplicity involved in waiting for a kettle to boil or a bus to arrive, to the emotion wrapped around the wait for a much-loved friend to step on to the platform from a cross-country train or a phone call that might contain the news we dread…

'As we embark on the waiting period that is the Advent season, stretching to Christmas and a few days beyond, we'll discover why we're asked to wait, what we should be doing while we wait, and ultimately what we are waiting for. We can begin to see how God uses our everyday waiting times to parallel the journey that is our spiritual life…'

ISBN 1 84101 296 3   £6.99
Available from your local Christian bookshop or, in case of difficulty, direct from BRF using the order form on page 221.

HOPE IN THE WILDERNESS

Bible readings from Advent to Epiphany

David Winter

'The world has many stories. Some make us laugh, some make us cry, some we forget and others we remember all our lives. But there are a few, very few, that mirror the human experience so vividly and completely that they have themselves become part of that experience. This book retells and reflects on perhaps the greatest of them all, the Exodus—the story of a group of men and women, with a charismatic but flawed leader, making their way from slavery in Egypt to a promised land "flowing with milk and honey".

'It is also a story with profound meaning for many people at the personal level. I began this book while my wife was ill in hospital and completed it in the first year of a painful bereavement. For me it became the story of a slow and arduous journey through a barren and desolate landscape towards a place of distant promise.'

Follow the story with David Winter, in this book of Bible readings and comment for every day in the season of Advent and Christmas, and discover how we too, like the people of Israel long ago, live under the justice and mercy of God.

ISBN 1 84101 258 0   £6.99
Available from your local Christian bookshop or, in case of difficulty, direct from BRF using the order form on page 221.

LIGHTED WINDOWS

An Advent calendar for a world in waiting

Margaret Silf

The world waits—sometimes holding its breath in fear of what tomorrow may bring, sometimes in a haze of busyness, or boredom, in which we hardly know what we are waiting for. Yet we still wait in hopefulness. The birth of a baby invariably stirs deep wells of hope in the human heart. Perhaps in this generation, things will get better. Perhaps this child will make a difference.

As we approach the Christmas season we prepare to celebrate the coming to earth of someone who really does make a difference. At this season the 'windows' of our human experience can change from rows of faceless panes, perhaps grimy with dirt, into lighted windows that open up new possibilities and coax us into a place where rejoicing might be possible.

The journey mapped out in this book is an invitation to look into some of these lighted windows, and discover a few reflections of what we wait for, and long for—reflections of God's guidance, his call to trust him and live by his wisdom.

ISBN 1 84101 255 6   £6.99
Available from your local Christian bookshop or, in case of difficulty, direct from BRF using the order form on page 221.

You may be interested to know that Gordon Giles is a regular contributor to *New Daylight*, BRF's popular series of Bible reading notes. *New Daylight* is ideal for those looking for a fresh, devotional approach to reading and understanding the Bible. Each issue covers four months of daily Bible reading and reflection with each day offering a Bible passage (text included), helpful comment and a prayer or thought for the day ahead.

New Daylight is also available in large print and on cassette for the visually impaired.

NEW DAYLIGHT SUBSCRIPTIONS

❏ I would like to give a gift subscription
   (please complete both name and address sections below)
❏ I would like to take out a subscription myself
   (complete name and address details only once)

This completed coupon should be sent with appropriate payment to BRF. Alternatively, please write to us quoting your name, address, the subscription you would like for either yourself or a friend (with their name and address), the start date and credit card number, expiry date and signature if paying by credit card.

Gift subscription name _____

Gift subscription address _____

_____ Postcode _____

Please send to the above, beginning with the next January/May/September issue: (delete as applicable)

(please tick box)	UK	SURFACE	AIR MAIL
NEW DAYLIGHT	❏ £11.70	❏ £13.05	❏ £15.30
NEW DAYLIGHT 3-year sub	❏ £29.25		

Please complete the payment details below and send your coupon, with appropriate payment to: **BRF, First Floor, Elsfield Hall, 15–17 Elsfield Way, Oxford OX2 8FG**

Your name _____

Your address _____

_____ Postcode _____

Total enclosed £ _____ (cheques should be made payable to 'BRF')

Payment by cheque ❏ postal order ❏ Visa ❏ Mastercard ❏ Switch ❏

Card number: ⬚⬚⬚⬚⬚⬚⬚⬚⬚⬚⬚⬚⬚⬚⬚⬚⬚⬚⬚⬚

Expiry date of card: ⬚⬚⬚⬚ Issue number (Switch): ⬚⬚⬚⬚

Signature (essential if paying by credit/Switch card)_____

❏ Please do not send me further information about BRF publicaations.

NB: BRF notes are also available from your local Christian bookshop.   **BRF is a Registered Charity**

Resourcing your spiritual journey

through...

- Bible reading notes
- Books for Advent & Lent
- Books for Bible study and prayer
- Books to resource those working with
  under 11s in school, church and at home

- Quiet days and retreats
- Training for primary teachers
  and children's leaders
- Godly Play
- Barnabas Live

For more information, visit the **brf** website at **www.brf.org.uk**